Praise for Sharon Good and
Creative Marketing Tools for Coaches

"Where was Sharon Good and *Creative Marketing Tools for Coaches* when I started my company? Sharon's do-it-yourself approach and practical advice for marketing a coaching practice is essential for the new coach entering the marketplace and is also valuable and thought provoking for the seasoned coach with a successful practice."

Brian Kurth, President of Brian Kurth + Company
and VocationVacations

"What a great idea to use marketing tools that you enjoy! This book is a coaches' dream — clear, concise, and step-by-step. But should I let it out that *Creative Marketing Tools for Coaches* has a broader audience than just coaches? Any infopreneur will benefit from these marketing techniques, as Sharon skillfully guides you through deciding on and implementing your marketing strategy."

Marina Spence, Author of *Make Every Day a Friday!
The Joy of Connecting Who You Are with What You Do*

"Are you skilled as a coach, but at a loss when it comes to marketing yourself? Do terms like 'niche,' 'brand' and 'target market' sound intimidating? Let *Creative Marketing Tools for Coaches* be your gentle guide. It speaks to you in the voice of a deep and caring marketing maven who wants you to not only thrive in your business, but also to enjoy the journey. Every time you open the book, it's like having a conversation with Sharon Good over coffee — just the two of you sitting in her study surrounded by a world of marketing wisdom. And she makes it all about you. What more could you ask for?"

Nancy Ancowitz, Business Communication Coach
and Author of *Self-Promotion for Introverts*®

"With all the Internet tools now available, marketing has never before presented more opportunities for the coach/entrepreneur. But the complexity can be overwhelming. Without a roadmap, building a successful coaching business is a bumpy journey. Sharon Good's resource book, *Creative Marketing Tools for Coaches*, takes the mystery out of marketing, breaking the process down into comprehensive steps and options. She shows how coaches can succeed, even if we're not great at public speaking, writing or networking. It allows me to feel newly empowered with the realization that I can take control of the destiny of my coaching business."

Bonnie Mincu, Senior Certified ADHD Coach, Thrive with ADD

"Sharon's book should be the bible for any coach building a practice! I only wish I had this resource when I started out 10 years ago. Even now, I found myself copying resources and ideas from the book. Don't waste time making mistakes on your own, or fretting about what to do. Walk — no run — and buy this book!"

Dale Kurow, MS, Executive Coach

"An invaluable, step-by-step guide that demystifies the marketing and branding process for coaches. A must-read for new and experienced coaches alike!"

Marianna Lead, PhD, Founder of Goal Imagery® Coaching

"*Creative Marketing Tools for Coaches* is a comprehensive, easy-to-read guide for new and experienced coaches. Use it to kick start your business or take your marketing efforts to the next level. Whether you want to create a website, write a book, start blogging or get out and network, this is an in-depth resource for marketing success. I will recommend it to all my coach trainees!"

Jodi Sleeper-Triplett, MCC, SCAC; JST Coaching, LLC;
Premiere Coach Training & Coaching Company

"This book is for any coach who wants to learn how to create and use marketing tools to attract their target audience. Sharon's sage advice makes it easy for you to identify and use the best marketing tools available no matter where you're starting."

Paulette Rao, MCC, Founder, True North Resources,
Conscious Coaching Institute

"As a Sensitive, I tend to shy away from marketing books because of the hard-sell energy. But I loved *Creative Marketing Tools for Coaches*! Its easy, relaxed tone grounds me and keeps me focused on BEing myself as a way to attract coaching clients. I never once went into overwhelm while exploring the incredible amount of information Sharon provides for each tool. Thank you so much for modeling sensitive marketing!"

Carolyn Wilson-Elliott, Author of *Survival Guide for Empaths,
Clairsentients & Highly Sensitive Persons*

"As a Professional Life and Career Coach, Sharon has an innate ability to help and guide individuals to reach their highest potential. Sharon's dedication to personal and professional development, as well as her ability to formulate results with clients, make Sharon a sought after Life and Career Coach. As the Lead Life and Career Coach with VocationVacations, it's been my pleasure to work with Sharon. Her dedication to her work is evident in everything she does."

Will Wiebe, CPC, Lead Life/Career Coach, VocationVacations

Creative MARKETING TOOLS *for* COACHES

Use Your Natural Gifts to Attract Your Ideal Clients

Sharon Good

Good Life Press

New York

Published by:
Good Life Press, a division of
Good Life Coaching Inc.
New York, New York
www.goodlifecoaching.com
www.goodlifepress.com

Disclaimer: Any resources mentioned in this book are for information only. The author and publisher accept no responsibility for the reader's experience with any product or vendor and advise the reader to personally evaluate any resource they are considering purchasing or utilizing.

Publishers Cataloging in Publication Data
(Provided by Quality Books Inc.)

Good, Sharon.
   Creative marketing tools for coaches : use your natural gifts to attract your ideal clients / Sharon Good.
   p. cm.
   LCCN 2009900619
   ISBN-13: 978-0-9823172-0-4
   ISBN-10: 0-9823172-0-4
   ISBN-13: 978-0-9823172-1-1
   ISBN-10: 0-9823172-1-2

   1. Personal coaching--Marketing. 2. Executive coaching--Marketing.   I. Title.

BF637.P36G66 2009   158'.3'068
                      QBI09-600053

Cover design by Justine Elliott

Printed in the United States of America

*This book is dedicated to my family
—mom Selma, sister Bonnie and cousin Irene—
who are always there to support me.*

CONTENTS

SECTION III: OTHER WAYS TO MARKET

Acknowledgments

While writing a book is a solo journey, there are many people who support the author behind the scenes.

I'd like to thank my mentors, Fern Gorin and Linda Manassee Buell, who taught me the basics of marketing.

Colleagues who encouraged and supported me in developing my materials into a course at New York University, which later became this book: Elizabeth Guilday, Stephen Cluney, Howard Greenstein, Paulette Rao and Erika Levasseur. Also Renate Reimann, who went from student to colleague and offered valuable feedback on the manuscript.

My friend and editor, Shanna Richman, who is always supportive and honest.

Friends who've been there always: Jim Shewalter, Maria Ciaccia, Barnet Shindlman, Michael Dubin and the Light Group (you know who you are).

My professional support group and dear friends: Jane Cranston, Dale Kurow and Bonnie Mincu.

My family, who don't always understand what I do, but are always there to love and support me.

PREFACE

When I started my coaching practice in 1997, naïve as I was, I expected to hang my shingle and have clients come knocking at my door. It didn't quite happen that way. Even if you believe in the Law of Attraction, say all the right affirmations, have a vision board and are open to "receiving" clients, there are still things you have to do.

Marketing is a necessary "evil" for anyone in private practice. Like many professionals, coaches may be great at what they do, but lack the skills to market effectively. Or they know what to do, but they're uncomfortable, or even terrified, about getting out there, presenting themselves as professionals and asking for business.

Marketing is most effective when you target your efforts and do them consistently. The best way to do this is to choose marketing strategies that call upon your gifts and strengths — things you like to do anyway.

This book includes an array of marketing tools that you can choose from. You'll learn what they are, their benefits and how you can begin implementing them. Through trial and error, you'll find the ones that work best for you.

You don't have to be a high-powered salesperson to have a successful coaching practice. Work with your marketing tools regularly and consistently, and over time, momentum will build and clients will seek you out.

INTRODUCTION

This book is designed to provide an overview of the various tools available to you, as a coach, to market your practice and reach prospective clients. Coverage of each topic is not meant to be comprehensive. Rather, my intention here is to give you an overview of the selection of tools available and provide enough information for you to make an informed decision about which tools would be most effective for you.

Use this book to explore what's possible, and which tools best fit with your gifts and talents. Then, use the Resources at the back of each chapter, as well as your own path of discovery, to learn and use the tools with greater depth.

How to Use This Book

This book is meant to be treated as a toolbox. Ultimately, you can use it as a reference tool as you develop your marketing strategies. Initially, I recommend reading through the entire book to get a full overview of the various tools that you can select. You may find that a tool you hadn't considered at first is attractive to you when you learn more about it.

Section I: Getting Prepared gives you the foundation upon which your tools will rest. You'll clarify your niche and target market, your marketing message and your brand, as well as learning how coaches market themselves.

Section II: The Tools is the meat of the book. You'll learn about each of the tools — its benefits and how to get started and work with it. Each chapter also includes resources for further exploring that tool.

Section III: Other Ways to Market points out other strategies you can add to your marketing toolkit. The Closing Notes pull it all together and remind you how you can use this book to greatest advantage.

Once you've gotten the overview, use the Strategy worksheet in Appendix F to select the tools that most appeal to you and the order in which you want to implement them. The philosophy I follow is that if you choose tools that appeal to you, you're more likely to use them on a regular basis — an important part of effective marketing.

If you love to write, you might want to start with an e-zine or write articles for magazines, newspapers or to post on the Web. If being in front of an audience excites you, speaking, workshops, podcasts and media appearances would be just the thing for you. If you enjoy designing and developing materials, go for the website and promotional materials. As a people person, networking and connecting with referral sources would come naturally for you. If you're an introvert, writing books or communicating via a blog could work well for you.

You also want to consider which tools will be most effective in reaching your target market. Think about how your potential clients access information, and select your tools accordingly. If you want to work with older retirees, a blog or podcast wouldn't be your best choice. You might consider instead writing articles for print media or offering seminars. While technology, and particularly social networking on the Web, has been exploding as a way of connecting with young people and business professionals, face-to-face contact is always the most effective with any audience.

Take your time, both reading the book and implementing the tools. Don't try to take on too much at one time. In your first reading, you might want to skip over the exercises and come back to them later. When you're ready, begin by doing the exercises in Section I to clarify who you're marketing to, what you want to say to them and how you want to present yourself.

Next, use Appendix F, My Creative Marketing Strategy, to rate the level of appeal that each tool has for you and the order in which you want to work with them. Think about which tools would be the easiest for you and/or get you the quickest results. As a rule, I would recommend that everyone have at least a simple website or blog, although you don't have to start there. You can begin with a basic business card that you can use for networking or approaching referral sources. In the long term, though, having a Web presence gives you professional credibility and makes you accessible to a wider range of clients outside your local area.

Select two or three tools to start. You might begin writing articles while you develop your website and create a list of workshop titles. You'll find that the material you develop for one tool will also inform your other tools — this is part of consistent branding (see chapter 3). Don't be afraid to use the same concepts, expressed in various ways, across your range of marketing tools.

Give your ideas time to germinate and evolve. You may target two months for completing your website, but find your ideas aren't gelling that quickly. The beauty of a website is that you can put up some basic material and then continue building and modifying it over time. The same is true for other tools. Start with what you've got, test it out and allow your ideas to emerge and evolve through experience. Don't wait until everything is "perfect" to get yourself out there and connect with potential clients. Start where you can and continue developing your tools over time.

Use the exercises in each chapter to help you think through the process. Start with the exercises in Section I to build your foundation. Then, work with the exercises for the tools you've selected. Work with one exercise at a time. Write it out, then put it away and come back to it in a day or two. Allow your ideas to develop over several sittings. Then, take action on what you've learned.

Be sure to set aside time each week for marketing. Over time — and I'm talking years here, not weeks or months — try out a variety of tools and see which ones are most effective for you. It's different for each person, so I can't give you a formula. Through trial and error, you'll discover your best marketing strategy.

Feel free to experiment. You may be surprised to find that a tool that was challenging for you at first, such as public speaking, becomes your favorite. Find the tools that work best for you, and add new ones once the old ones are running smoothly.

In the beginning, you'll spend more time testing out marketing strategies as you build your coaching practice. As you move forward, your strategies will gain momentum, and you'll spend more time coaching while your well-established marketing tools are out there doing the job for you.

Exploring the Resources

At the back of each chapter, there are several suggested resources for exploring and implementing that tool. In this age of information, these are merely a drop in the bucket of resources available. Use these as a starting point, and continue researching your favorite tools in bookstores, on the Internet and out in the field.

Keep in mind, too, that information, especially on the Internet, changes quickly. New resources are appearing all the time, and the older ones go out of date almost as soon as they're posted. Explore the resources listed here, and use keyword searches to find additional ones. Also, keep in mind that information on the Internet is not always reliable, so be sure to check things out for yourself.

Finally, have fun! After all, this is a key part of running your business, and your best marketing tool may be the enthusiasm you have for what you do.

So, let's get started!

Section I:
GETTING PREPARED

 **ONE**

CLARIFYING YOUR NICHE
AND TARGET MARKET

Before you choose which marketing tools will be most effective for you, it's important to clarify *who* you'll be marketing to. How you communicate your message to a 20-year-old college student is different from speaking to someone who's on the verge of becoming a parent, entering midlife or approaching retirement. You'll speak differently to an artist, a scientist or a banker.

In a market that is continually becoming more competitive, it's also important to create a distinct identity, or brand image, for yourself, so that your target market will be able to find you.

While it may seem that by having a broader identity, you'll reach more people, the opposite is true. For starters, you don't want to reach *everybody* — you don't want to waste your precious time and energy speaking to people who want a completely different type of coach. You want to reach your *ideal* client. Creating a clear identity will help the right clients find you.

Many coaches are multifaceted. They want to be able to use a variety of skills and work with different types of clients. Even so, you need to present a clear identity to the world. Once you begin working with a client, you can pull out your bag of tricks. You can even list all the different coaching niches and services you offer on your marketing materials as features of your coaching.

Think of it this way: Imagine that you're walking through a shopping mall looking for a vacuum cleaner. As you pass each shop window, it's filled with hundreds of products. Then, you spot a window that clearly features vacuum cleaners. Which one would you be more likely to enter? Probably the one that prominently features what you're looking for. Then, once inside the store, you may find many more interesting things to buy.

Your Coaching Focus

Your coaching focus includes two things: your niche and your target market. Your **niche** is the *type* of coaching you'll do. Some common niches include:

◆ personal or life coaching
◆ corporate, organizational or executive coaching
◆ relationship coaching
◆ career coaching
◆ wellness coaching
◆ transition coaching
◆ small business coaching
◆ sales coaching
◆ spiritual coaching

Your **target market** is *who* you'll coach, such as:

◆ women 25 to 45
◆ new divorcees
◆ mid-life adults who are into spiritual development
◆ single working parents
◆ C-level executives (CEOs, CFOs, etc.)

... and many others.

If your coaching practice includes more than one niche and/or target market, look for a unifying concept. For example, if you're working with college students getting their first job, people in midlife making a career change, and retirees moving into active retirement, you might call yourself a Career Transition Coach. If you're working with corporate refugees starting a consulting business and stay-at-home moms who want to start a home-based business, you might be an Entrepreneurial Coach.

EXERCISE
Finding Your Coaching Niche and Target Market

Let's do an exercise to begin defining your coaching niche and target market. Start by writing your answers to the following questions.

1. **What are my strengths and skills? In what areas, careers or industries do I have experience and expertise?**

   This can be from professional or personal experience. Include only skills that you enjoy using or that you are willing to use, not the ones you hate.

2. **What experiences have I had personally in which I can support others?**

   Have you successfully navigated a health issue? Have you been a single parent, or has your child faced a challenge? Have you learned how to do something that others would want to learn?

3. **What are my passions? What do I love to talk about? Read about? Study?**

   Do you love talking about business? Personal growth? Spirituality? Health?

4. **What kinds of people do I enjoy being around and working with?**

    You'll be spending a lot of time with your coaching clients. What kinds of people do you find enjoyable and stimulating? Who do you want to avoid (e.g., chronic complainers)?

5. **How do I want to impact those people? What impact do I want to have on the world?**

    Do you feel a calling to help people find careers they love? Help women build self-esteem? Help people live healthier lives? Help working parents have a more balanced life? Support young couples in having successful marriages and families? Guide artists to have lucrative careers?

6. **How much do I want to charge for my services? Can my target audience pay this rate?**

    If your goal is to make six figures, working with young artists might not get you the level of income you want. Ask yourself, Is your income level more important than working with people in an area you're passionate about? Is there a way to have both? Could you have a passion niche and a money niche?

7. **What will keep me in flow? Challenged and engaged?**

    According to psychologist Mihaly Csikszentmihalyi, "flow" occurs when optimal levels of challenge and skill intersect. How can you design your coaching practice so that you feel optimally challenged? What do you need to do to keep it fresh and interesting for yourself? Do you need to develop a new niche every few years? Do you need to continually enhance your skills?

Look at your responses to the above questions and make a list of the key elements that will help define your coaching niche. Include the following:

- the types of people you want to work with
- topics you want to address
- skills you could share
- types of coaching you want to do
- a passion or purpose you need to fulfill
- your income requirements
- anything you need to include to remain engaged and stimulated, to forward your own growth and development as a person and a coach

Finally, list your top one to three niches. Be specific. For example:
- Career coaching with creative artists (That's mine!)
- Executive coaching with top level executives in the financial services industry
- Life coaching with twenty-somethings who want to get their life and career on track

1. _____
2. _____
3. _____

If you have more than three niches, go ahead and list them. As you're working with clients, see which ones "rise to the top."

Now that you've gotten more clarity about who you're going to coach, and on what, the next step to get clear on is what to say to them!

 **Two**

Clarifying Your Message

Many new coaches have difficulty explaining what they do. Much of the general public still doesn't have a clear picture of what coaching is or how it works. If they do know, they may see it as a luxury they can't afford.

Those of us in the business know that coaching offers huge benefits to people, and it is our job to formulate our message so that we can clearly communicate that value to those who might want to reap those benefits.

What do you want to communicate to potential clients?

While the term "life coach" is becoming popularized in the media, there's still a vague image out there about what coaches actually do. Many of the portrayals in the media are misleading, often crossing the line and portraying coaching as counseling or making coaching look silly.

In order to make new coaching clients comfortable, you need to be able to communicate exactly what you do with your clients and why people should plunk down their hard-earned money to work with you in particular. In sales jargon, this is called Features and Benefits.

Features

Features describes what you do and how you do it. This includes such things as:

◆ What type of coaching you do
◆ How you work with clients
◆ What actually happens in a coaching session
◆ What types of coaching processes you use
◆ How long is the session and how often do you meet
◆ How long is a typical coaching engagement
◆ What other skills or services you make available to clients, such as business consulting, nutrition counseling, different forms of healing, career assessments, resume writing, presentation skills, etc.

Benefits

Although people want to know about your Features, what they buy is your Benefits. Benefits are what people get from working with you. Will they advance in their career? Increase their income? Have better relationships? Get support in successfully starting their business? Clean up their act and have a happier life? Finally achieve that goal or complete that project they've been stuck on for years?

The best way to demonstrate benefits is with success stories. What are some of the benefits your clients have achieved from working with you? Always be prepared with a few anecdotes to share when you're networking, doing a workshop or writing an article.

Since at least some of your marketing will be done on the Internet, start to think about keywords. If someone is doing a Google search, what are some of the keywords that will bring up your website? Some examples are:

- business success
- starting a business
- better relationships
- work I love
- life coach
- career coach
- balanced lifestyle
- better health
- lose weight, etc.

EXERCISE
Your Features and Benefits

- **Make a list of your "features" — the services you offer.**

  This should include specific types of coaching you do, as well as any other services you're qualified to offer, such as financial planning, nutrition counseling, writing business plans, NLP (neuro-linguistic programming), healing modalities such as massage or Reiki, etc.

- **What are the benefits of working with you?**

  How will clients' lives improve as a result of working with you? How can you help them get something they want or ease their pain?

Remember — you need to be specific about what you offer. Saying, "I can coach you on anything," doesn't give your potential client anything to grab onto that they can relate to.

Stating Your Message

Now that you're clear on what you're offering, you need to articulate that in different ways. You'll do this through your website and printed materials, as well as through verbal communication.

One of the best ways I've found to figure out how to articulate your message is to start writing your Web pages or a brochure. Look at it from the perspective of a potential client. What is it they need to know to be sure (or at least suspect) that 1) coaching is the right path for them and 2) you're the right coach for them?

It's also important to be able to speak comfortably about what you do when you meet people in person. Clarifying your Features and Benefits will certainly help you do that. It's also helpful to be prepared with a Sound Byte, also called an Elevator Speech.

Sound Byte

The concept of a Sound Byte is that with this compact device, you can tell someone enough about what you do for them to be intrigued and ask for your business card, or more information, in the 20 to 30 seconds you spend with them on an elevator.

Imagine you meet someone and they ask you what you do. You reply, "I'm a Life Coach." Their response might be, "Oh, yeah, I've heard about that on TV." Not much energy there.

Now, imagine someone asks you that question and you say, "I help people make a living doing what they love," or "I help entrepreneurs to have a successful business and a balanced life." Wouldn't that grab your attention? Wouldn't you want to hear more?

EXERCISE
Communicating Your Message

How can you communicate your message to potential clients? How would you tell a potential client what you do?

1. **Review your work from chapter 1.**

   Who is your target market? Your coaching niche?

   What is it that this group wants or needs in order to have a better life / career / relationships / health / etc.?

   What pain would you be alleviating by being their coach?

2. **In looking at question 1, as well as your Features and Benefits, what are some phrases and keywords that your target audience will respond to?**

   If someone was searching for a coach on the Internet, what words or phrases would lead them to you?

3. **Write and try out a Sound Byte (aka Elevator Speech).**

   Come up with several versions. If you have more than one niche or target audience, include at least one version for each. Look for opportunities to try out your sound bytes, see which ones work best and further refine them.

ADDITIONAL EXERCISES

1. **Write copy for a brochure.** (see chapter 13)
2. **Write copy for your Web pages.** (see chapter 5)

What keywords would you use? Remember to include your Features and Benefits.

Next, we're going to use what you've learned so far to begin creating your personal brand.

THREE

CREATING YOUR BRAND

"Brand" is a buzz word that's used a lot these days. In the past, it referred to the corporate image and product lines of big companies, such as Kellogg's™ or Colgate® or Chevrolet™. Now, even small business owners — and solopreneurs like yourself — need to create a unique presentation for themselves. That is your brand.

Your brand includes such things as:

◆ Your business name

◆ Your logo

◆ Your title and coaching specialty(s) — what you're known for

◆ The way you present yourself in all your materials, from your website to your stationery and business card. This includes the design features and colors you use — when you see a red and white bull's-eye, don't you think of Target®? When you see the "swoosh" on the side of a sneaker (or anywhere, for that matter), don't you think, "Nike"? When I see orange and turquoise together, the Howard Johnson® hotels and restaurants still come to mind.

Creating a Professional Image

Let's begin by looking at how you want to present yourself. Depending on who you're trying to reach, you would present yourself in a different way. If you were seeking a job in a music store, you would dress differently than you would pursuing a job on Wall Street.

In the same way, if you're an Executive Coach marketing to human resource managers, your presentation will be very different from a Life Coach marketing to working moms or a Wellness Coach marketing to middle-aged adults. If your target audience is corporations, your materials will need a slicker, more institutional look than if you're targeting individuals. You will need to approach 20-somethings differently than 50-somethings. If you're targeting men, your materials will have a different look and feel than they would if you're primarily targeting women.

EXERCISE
What image do you want to project?

1. Make a list of adjectives describing the image and tone you want to convey to your target audience.

    Here are some examples:
    - Super-professional
    - Competent
    - Friendly
    - Knowledgeable
    - Healthy
    - Reliable
    - Supportive
    - Empathetic
    - Experienced
    - Open

2. **How do you want to leave people feeling when they read your materials?**

   Here are some examples:
   - Hopeful
   - Energized
   - Excited
   - Fearful
   - Motivated
   - Curious
   - Interested
   - That they've found the answer to their problem
   - That they need me!

   If you have more than one target audience, make a list for each one. How alike or different are those lists? Based on this information, will you need to present yourself differently for each target group?

   ❧

In designing your materials, don't feel you have to follow the pack. There are many ways to present yourself and your business. It's important to include yourself in your materials. Let your personality and approach come through. When you express yourself authentically through your website, your brochure and business card, you're more likely to attract the clients you'll resonate with — and more likely to retain them.

In addition, let your unique style be reflected in your personal presentation: the way you dress and present yourself to clients. Do you want to appear in suits or more casually? Will you dress in bright colors or somber tones?

By coordinating your materials and your personal presentation, you'll have a consistent, unified "look" that clients will remember.

Your Business Name

You can also strategically choose your business name to support your brand. In choosing a business name, you can take one of these approaches:

- Create a name using your name, such Jane Jones Coaching or Jones Coaching and Consulting.
- Use a unique business name, such as New Futures Life Coaching or Innovative Leadership Institute.
- Use an identifiable phrase, such Find Your Passion Life Coaching or Ideal Career Coaching.

Your Domain Name (aka Web Address or URL)

With the predominance of the Internet as a way for people to find you, you will also need to check the availability of your chosen domain name. Your domain name may be the same as your business name or a variation.

Some examples:

- Using your name: www.janejonescoaching.com
- Using a company name: www.newfutureslifecoaching.com or www.innovativeleadership.biz
- Using an identifiable phrase: www.findyourpassion.com or www.idealcareercoaching.com

You can test to see if a domain name is already taken by using one of the following methods:

- Enter the name on your Web browser and see if a website comes up. You may see a notice that the website is "under construction." That means it's taken, but the owner hasn't yet put up their pages.
- Do a "whois" search at www.whois.com. Also, many of the sites where you can register domains and purchase Web hosting allow you to search to see whether your desired domain name is still

available. With a "whois" search, you can also find out if alternative suffixes are available besides .com, such as .net, .org or .biz, among others.

I would recommend that you determine and reserve your domain name *before* finalizing a business name. The same business name can be registered in different states, but there's only one Internet.

Your Title

Your title as a coach also supports your brand. It will most likely reflect the type of coaching you do.

- Life Coach (or Personal Coach)
- Career Coach
- Executive Coach
- Health and Wellness Coach
- Transition Coach
- Retirement Coach
- Spiritual Coach
- Relationship Coach

You can also use a combination that better reflects your niche and specialties. For example, my title is Life, Career and Creativity Coach. (I would limit it to three niches at most.) You can also come up with something creative and attention-getting that's appropriate for your target audience, such as a Fun Coach or a Mid-Life Transitions Coach.

EXERCISE 1
Brainstorm Your Business Name and Web Address

Brainstorming is a great process for coming up with a business name. Try these steps:

1. Create a list of keywords and phrases that inspire you or reflect the tone you want to communicate. Use some of the words you

came up with in previous exercises, as well as new ones. Use a thesaurus to generate additional ideas.

2. Get together with one or more colleagues or friends and toss around ideas. Come up with a list of five to ten business names that you like.

3. Test out domain names, to make sure your desired names are available. Try different combinations of words, as well as using hyphens (e.g., www.sharon-good.com) and different suffixes (.com, .net, .biz, etc.). Eliminate any names that don't work.

4. Test out your list of ideas on other friends and colleagues, and especially those who might represent your target audience, to come up with your best option.

5. Register your domain name! (See chapter 5.)

EXERCISE 2
Brainstorm Your Business Title

Come up with a title for yourself, using the niches you defined for yourself in chapter 1. Some examples are: Life Coach, Career Coach, Executive Coach, Wellness Coach, Transitions Coach, etc. Your title may combine two or three key niches (e.g., Personal and Business Coach). If you're not sure, brainstorm several ideas and test them out on friends and colleagues. Try the exercise above, and also look at other coaches' websites for ideas.

Try out your new business name and title for awhile and see how they work for you. It's easy enough to change your website or print new business cards to reflect the evolution of your business.

Now that you've got your identity as a coach, let's look at how you can apply that to best market your coaching business.

Four

How Do Coaches Market Themselves?

Many solo and small business professionals are great at what they do, but find marketing a challenge. Even if you have a background in corporate marketing, it's a different ballgame marketing yourself. That's why agents were invented!

But since coaches don't have agents, we need to face the challenge of doing it ourselves. The good news is, we can do it in ways we enjoy.

Some Concepts

Before we get into the nuts and bolts of marketing, I'd like to begin with a few key concepts.

Make a Personal Connection

Because coaching is a personal service, it's best sold through personal connection. The rule of thumb for a marketing tool is, the closer you are in contact with your audience, the more effective it will be.

Many new coaches feel shy about speaking about their services, so they lean toward marketing tools that don't require them to be present, such as newspaper ads and brochures. Few people connect with coaches from ads, unless they're placed in publications that are highly targeted for your niche, placed in a prominent position and run numerous times. This can become costly, and it doesn't give you a great return on your investment.

Ads can be effective when you're promoting a specific event, such as a workshop. Brochures are a handy tool to supplement other activities, but not the best as a primary marketing activity.

The most effective types of marketing are the kind where you can actually meet your prospective clients face-to-face and give them an experience of you. Doing presentations and workshops tops the list here. You can also be effective with different forms of writing, such as articles, e-zines and books. You can even show your personality on your website and use it to let clients know who you are.

Use Multiple Approaches

Over time, you'll find a particular combination of marketing tools that work very well for you. In the beginning, though, I recommend trying out a variety of approaches. Years ago, when I co-founded a book publishing company, I learned from a marketing expert that you'll get 80% of your business from 20% of your marketing ... but you won't necessarily know which 20% it is!

Different types of marketing may be more or less effective for different coaches, depending on your personality, your talents and your target audiences. Also, which tools are most effective may shift as times change.

As you go through this book, pick out three or four tools that you would enjoy working with. Start with one or two, and add in a couple more as time permits. Start small and test them out. By experimenting, you'll see which ones bring you the best results. Try some tools that are intriguing, but a stretch for you—you may be surprised at how well they work and how much you enjoy them!

Offer Different Levels of Products and Services

For many people, coaching is a big ticket item. By offering options, you can bring clients into the fold and allow them to try out your work and your philosophies in a small way first. There are two approaches to this:

♦ **Offer introductory products, such as books, audios and short classes that give clients the opportunity to become familiar with your work and experience how it helps them**

You may fear that this will take away clients. Chances are that some people will not have any intention of springing for private coaching, but they will purchase affordable self-study programs. Once they've tried these, though, they may realize that they can't do it alone and see the value in contacting you for help.

♦ **Have different levels of coaching programs**

For example, you might have a Gold Level program that offers four hours of coaching a month for $500, a Silver Level with three hours for $400, and a Bronze Level with two hours for $300. You can also offer bonuses at each level, such as copies of your books and audios, assessment tools, etc. You might even offer group coaching at a lower rate as an entry-level program.

Your Natural Marketing Style

An important part of marketing is doing it consistently. If you hate doing it, you won't, or you'll do it sporadically. The approach I favor is to choose marketing tools that you will enjoy doing for their own sake, so that you will be comfortable, and even enjoy doing them on a regular basis.

If you're a ham (like me!) and enjoy being in front of an audience, speaking and teaching would be great tools for you. You might also enjoy doing audios, videos, radio shows or podcasts.

If you love writing, you could choose to do books, e-books, e-zines, blogs, articles and other written materials.

If you're a people person, networking might be your cup of tea.

If you love creating materials, you could have fun putting together websites, brochures, flyers, e-books and PowerPoint presentations.

If you love coaching (which you do or you wouldn't be reading this book!), doing sample sessions, groups or teleclasses could attract clients into your practice.

Throughout this book, we'll look at the many tools you can use to market yourself that will express your natural abilities and be fun for you, as well as effective. Try them out, and make choices that you'll be happy to do consistently. Use the worksheet in appendix F to evaluate your choices.

Where to Reach Your Target Market

Before we delve into the marketing tools, let's look at where you'll be able to find your target audience.

EXERCISE
Reaching Your Market

You're going to make a two-column chart. List your target market(s) in the left-hand column. In the right-hand column, identify as many ways as you can come up with to reach each market. Look at:

◆ **Where do they hang out?**
  - Do they attend business networking meetings? Belong to professional associations? Go to health food stores?
  - Do they attend classes at adult learning centers? PTA meetings or parenting classes?
  - Would they belong to a men's or women's group or a youth group at their church or synagogue?
  - Do they frequent social networking groups or online chat rooms?

♦ **What do they read, watch or listen to? Where do they look for information?**
  – What types of books?
  – Which newspapers?
  – Any special interest or trade magazines?
  – Which websites do they frequent? Which blogs do they follow?
  – Do they listen to talk radio or podcasts? Which ones?
  – What shows do they watch?

List as many options as you can, and be as specific as you can. For example, name specific magazines that your audience would read, specific book genres they would be attracted to (e.g., "recovery" or "spiritual development," rather than "self-help"), which sections of the newspaper they would gravitate to, etc.

Target Market	How To Reach Them

Now that you've done all the groundwork, we're ready to start exploring the tools!

Section II:
THE TOOLS

FIVE

WEBSITES

Websites are important for every business. A website is an effective, inexpensive way to get your message out to thousands of people, whether you're working locally, nationally or globally. Whatever other marketing tools you choose, a website should be among them.

BENEFITS

◆ **Professional presence**

Your website announces your business to the world. In the past, having a business card and stationery established that you were in business. Nowadays, it's pretty much expected that any legitimate business will have a Web presence.

◆ **Let clients know who you are**

A website is a way to begin giving clients an experience of who you are. Along with your bio, you can include your philosophy or mission statement, articles you've written and testimonials from satisfied clients.

◆ **Credibility**

With identity fraud so rampant these days, having a website helps to give you credibility. Sure, information can be faked, but including information about yourself, your background, your credentials and your geographical location on the planet helps people to feel more secure before they hand over their credit card information and hundreds of dollars.

◆ **A 24/7 mega-brochure**

A website is available at all times. For a fraction of what it would cost to print a thousand small brochures, you can have dozens of pages of information and resources to inform potential clients about the value you can bring to them.

◆ **Reachability**

People look for services on the Internet more than any other source. With a website, along with good search engine optimization (SEO), potential clients can always find you.

◆ **Reach clients worldwide**

Since many coaches work by phone, the world is your market. You may have a specialty that's not readily available, or people may be drawn to your personal style, or you may be multilingual, and you may find yourself with clients all over the world.

GETTING STARTED

Defining Goals

Before you begin to write or design your website, it's important to define your goals—what you want your website to accomplish for you. You don't want to spend dozens of hours and thousands of dollars on a website, only to discover that you want to take your business in a completely different direction.

As you plan your website, think about how you can use it to reflect who you are and the types of clients you want to attract. People hire a person, not a business. They won't connect with a generic, institutional website that shows no signs of human life. Even if you use a do-it-yourself Web host, with standard templates, you can add text and graphics that show your personal style.

Many people are afraid to really put their personality into their website — they may feel they're too quirky — but that's what's going to attract the kinds of clients you want to work with. If you're doing executive coaching, then a slick, professional website makes sense. If you like working with artsy, creative people, you're not going to attract them with a buttoned-up, business-like website.

Think about the experience people will have when they come to your website, and design it appropriately. Think about what will entice them to read further, and show them who you are.

Let's begin by designing some goals for your coaching business and your website.

EXERCISE
Goals for Your Business and Your Website

1. **What is the purpose, vision or mission of your coaching business?**
   - Who do you want to serve? A particular group of people, life issue or industry?
   - What services do you want to offer? This includes the types of coaching you do as well as related services you're qualified to provide, such as nutrition counseling or career assessments.
   - How do you want to impact your clients? Do you want to help people have more meaningful and fulfilling lives and careers? Better work/life balance? More successful businesses?
   - What is your short-term and long-term vision? How do you want to grow personally, and how will that affect your business?

   For help in building a mission statement, try working with the Mission Statement Builder at the Franklin Covey website (www.franklincovey.com).

2. **How do you want to present yourself and your business?**
   - What image or tone do you want to present and project?
   - What is your business name? Your domain name? Your title as a coach?
   - What are three adjectives that describe the image and tone of your website? For example: friendly, professional, informative, inviting, etc.

Use the exercises in section I to further explore these areas.

3. **What is the purpose of your website?**
   - ❑ a 24/7 brochure
   - ❑ an administrative tool for managing clients
   - ❑ to create a mailing list or database
   - ❑ to share information and resources
   - ❑ to educate potential customers about what I do
   - ❑ to be a resource for my clients and the public
   - ❑ to generate more business
   - ❑ to update clients and prospects on my activities
   - ❑ to sell products and/or services online (e-commerce)
   - ❑ to enable people to register for classes
   - ❑ to create a community around my area(s) of focus
   - ❑ _____
   - ❑ _____
   - ❑ _____
   - ❑ _____
   - ❑ _____

4. **What actions do you want people to take?**
    ❑ learn more about me
    ❑ contact me by phone or e-mail for information
    ❑ make an appointment
    ❑ sign up for an introductory session
    ❑ buy a product or service
    ❑ subscribe to a newsletter
    ❑ register for a workshop
    ❑ participate in a blog or online community
    ❑ _____
    ❑ _____
    ❑ _____
    ❑ _____
    ❑ _____

Content

The content for your website should be aligned with your goals and objectives for your business and your website. Select the components that will best convey what you have to offer and support prospective clients in making the decision to hire you as their coach.

The following components should *always* be included:

◆ **Services and products you offer**

List the types of coaching you do, as well as any packages or programs you offer. (These are your Features—see chapter 2.) Many coaches also produce books, audios, workshops and other products as adjuncts to their coaching services. You can also include ancillary services that you are qualified to offer, such as resume writing, presentation skills, financial planning or healing services.

◆ Who you work with and the benefits you offer clients

Clients want to see themselves reflected on your website. Include text and graphics that convey who your ideal (or typical) client is, the types of issues they come to you to work on, as well as the benefits or results they'll get from working with you. (Go back to chapter 2 for a refresher on Benefits.)

◆ Biography / credentials

Unless the tone of your brand is highly institutional, and you want to give the impression that you have a large company with a myriad of people and resources, it's important to have a personal presence. Potential clients are more comfortable when they know who you are and what your background is. Even if you do want to present yourself as an institution, you can have a page about key staff.

You don't have to have a string of letters after your name, but people do want to know that you're qualified to coach them on their specific issues. Be sure to include formal education and degrees, as well as your coach training, professional background and life experiences that are relevant to your coaching focuses.

◆ Your picture

Remember, selling coaching is about people making a connection with you. Including an image of yourself makes it more personal.

◆ Pictures / graphics / logo

Graphics make your website more visually appealing, as well as contributing to the feeling you want to project and what you want to communicate to potential clients. A custom logo is a part of your branding.

◆ Contact information

It's important for potential clients to be able to find you. At the minimum, you should include a phone number, e-mail address and the city in which you're located. You can have a contact page, as well as including contact information at the bottom of every page.

With all the Internet fraud that's going on, it's important, for credibility, to include some indication of where you're located. For personal safety, unless you have a PO box, it's not necessary to include your street address. You might also want to have separate phone and fax numbers for your business. If you don't want to have a fax machine sitting in your office, you can use a virtual service, such as efax.com or callwave.com, to receive faxes.

◆ **Copyright**

While plagiarism from the Web is hard to keep track of, having a copyright can be a deterrent. Include a copyright statement on each page of your website, like this:

© 2009 Sharon Good. All rights in all media reserved.

Look at other websites, or even the copyright page of books, for other possible formats.

There are many other *optional* components and functions you might want to include in your website.

◆ **Your mission or philosophy**

This is a good way to let people know who you are, what your passions and principles are and how that is reflected in the way you work with your clients.

◆ **FAQs (frequency asked questions) / what is coaching**

Many people still don't know what coaching is or how it works, or they've been misinformed by TV comedies that portray coaching in a bad light. Use your website as an opportunity to educate them, let them know what to expect and perhaps draw new clients into coaching.

◆ **Pricing**

Some coaches include pricing on their website; others do not. Use your judgment on this. These are the two schools of thought around this:

- **Publish your pricing.** People want to know up front what your services will cost. If they can't afford your rates, they will "prescreen" themselves, and you won't spend precious time trying to enroll them. You might include pricing as part of your list of coaching programs.

- **Don't publish your pricing.** For many people, coaching is expensive, and seeing a price out of context might scare them away from something they could actually afford. Once they've spoken with you and see the value of coaching, the price won't seem so high and they're more likely to sign on. If you customize programs, you might want to let people know that you will speak with them individually, determine their needs and lay out a program before quoting a price.

◆ **Testimonials / success stories / client list**

People like to hear that you've successfully helped people with issues like theirs. It reassures them to know that you've worked with people like them and gotten positive results. If you're working with organizations, a client list also adds to your credibility.

◆ **Activities / events / classes**

Keep your audience apprised of any public appearances you will be making or classes you'll be offering. These events are a great way for potential clients to get an experience of you that can lead them to hire you as their coach, as well as providing additional income.

◆ **New products or services / special offers / news**

You can also keep people informed of any new products, services or time-limited specials you're offering. You can share news about yourself or anything relevant to your target audience — their interests, their industry, timely information, etc.

◆ **Articles**

If you write articles, you can post them on your website. It's a great way to give people an experience of you and get them in the door.

When interviewing prospective clients, I've had some of them tell me they spent an entire afternoon just reading my articles.

You can also submit articles elsewhere on the Web and have them link back to your website to make it more search-engine-friendly. (See chapter 9.)

◆ E-newsletter or e-zine

An e-newsletter, also called an e-zine, is a great way to build a mailing list, and you can post articles from past issues on your website. (See chapter 6.)

◆ Blog

Some people prefer the spontaneity and informality of a blog to writing a formal article or newsletter. It's also a great way to keep your website dynamic by continually adding new content. You can also invite "comments" to make it interactive. (See chapter 7.)

◆ Audio or video clips

New technology has made it very easy to produce and upload an audio or video clip. Be sparing with your use of media. Too many audio and video files can slow down the time it takes for your Web page to load and discourage people from visiting your site. (See chapter 11.)

◆ Resources and links

As an "added value" service, you can include book recommendations and links to information and complementary services that would be of interest to your target audience.

◆ E-commerce / ordering capability

Having e-commerce capability on your website allows people to order on the spot, when they're excited about your product or service. Ordering online is easy. If they have to call or mail something, they may decide not to bother.

◆ **Interactivity**

People love playing games and taking tests. Post a test that's relevant to your coaching niche. If the person gets a low score, it shows them that they need your services! You can also make your blog interactive or set up a chat room, to encourage people to return to your website on a regular basis.

◆ **Giveaways**

Offering something for free shows good will and gives people a sample of your work. You can offer a free introductory coaching session, a subscription to your newsletter, a report or e-booklet, etc.

◆ **Media page or "press room"**

If you're interested in doing interviews for newspapers or magazines, or in appearing on radio or television, you can use your media page to demonstrate your media experience by publishing or linking to past media coverage. You can also use this space to provide resources for the media, such as press releases, a fact sheet or bio, your areas of expertise and publishable pictures of yourself.

EXERCISE
Website Components

Select the different components or pages that you would like to include in your website.

- ✔ Services and products I offer
- ✔ Who I work with and benefits I offer clients
- ✔ Biography / credentials
- ✔ My picture
- ✔ Pictures / graphics / logo
- ✔ Contact information
- ✔ Copyright
- ❑ My mission or philosophy

❏ FAQs / what is coaching
❏ Pricing
❏ Testimonials / success stories / client list
❏ Activities / events / classes
❏ New products or services / special offers / news
❏ Articles
❏ E-newsletter or e-zine
❏ Blog
❏ Audio clips
❏ Video clips
❏ Resources and links
❏ E-commerce / ordering capability
❏ Interactive tests
❏ Giveaways
❏ Media page or "press room"
❏ _____
❏ _____
❏ _____
❏ _____
❏ _____

HOW TO WORK WITH WEBSITES

Managing Online Content

Let's begin by discussing the content of your website. While you may hire someone to write the copy, make sure that you have strong input in the content, so that it reflects your philosophy and personality. It's fine to write it yourself, but work with an editor to ensure that the final result is clean and professionally written, that it communicates the information and tone you intended and that there are no typos or grammatical errors.

Here are a few more guidelines to keep in mind when creating your Web content:

- Write your website content with the visitor in mind.
  - What kind of experience do you want them to have?
  - What information do you want to provide?
  - What action do you want to lead them to take?

- On the Web, less is more. Reading from a screen is hard on the eyes, so keep your copy short and succinct. Consider including about half of what you would for a printed document.

- Make it readable by breaking the text up into chunks. Have you ever tried to read 20 continuous lines of text on screen? It's mind-boggling!

- Use short subheads that describe what's coming, and use bullet points to break out lists.

- Make the copy catchy and enticing. As I mentioned above, it's harder to read from the screen, so you want to keep it engaging and easy.

- Update your content periodically to keep it fresh and dynamic. New material draws people back, and search engines love new content. Add articles, write a blog, update your events calendar, offer monthly specials, etc.

Planning Your Website

The design of your website should reflect your professional style and tone. Remember—when you express yourself authentically, you're more likely to attract the types of clients you want to work with.

EXERCISE
Describing Your Website

List five to ten adjectives or phrases you would use to describe the style and tone of your website. Some possibilities: professional, inviting, informative, friendly, exciting, enticing, motivating, empathetic ("this person gets me!"), corporate, nurturing, empowering, trustworthy, arty, techno, fun, healthy, beautiful, competent, etc.

Now that you've described what you want your website to project, let's look at some other aspects to keep in mind when planning your website.

◆ Your home page should be easy to navigate and not overloaded — less is definitely more. Visitors should be able to quickly determine who you are, what you're offering and how to locate specific topics and pages within your website.

◆ Your pages should be clear, consistent, attractive and inviting. Your website may be the first impression people have of you, and you want to make it a positive one. Even if you use a do-it-yourself Web host with standard templates, invest in a custom logo and graphics that reflect your brand and the tone you want to convey.

◆ Make your website easy to navigate. The design and structure should be consistent from one page to another. The navigation bar, which is usually on the top, the left or both, should have no more than five to seven headings. Include a navigation bar on every page — when someone goes to any page on your website, they should be able to get to other parts of the site without having to hit the Back button.

◆ Select colors that support your brand identity, and use them consistently throughout your website. Avoid dark, muddy-looking background colors. Choose type colors that stand out from the background, and make sure the type is big enough to be readable — especially if you're targeting an older audience.

◆ While it's fun to use high-tech stuff, like audios and videos, don't overdo it. Set it up so the user can start and stop the audio or video themselves — it can be embarrassing to be surfing the Web at work and click onto a page that automatically blares music or a verbal message.

◆ Make your pages easy to change and update. You can work with your Web designer/developer to do this, or have them teach you how to work with the software, so you can easily make changes yourself or assign this task to your assistant. If you use a do-it-yourself Web host, you'll also be able to do updates yourself.

◆ Guide users and make it easy for them to take the actions you want them to take. You can do this by the way you structure your navigation bars, as well as by using well-placed links or even a pop-up window that invites users to sign up for your mailing list or a special event.

Organizing Your Web Content

To begin planning your website, you can create a flow chart to give you a picture of how you want the information organized. As you plan, think of the user's experience, how they'll move through the site.

Start with broad category headings, such as:

◆ Home
◆ About Coaching
◆ Services
◆ How I Help Clients
◆ About the Coach
◆ Events Calendar
◆ Contact Us

From there, you can have sub-categories — either as a drop-down menu or as a new menu when you get to that page. For example, under Services, you might list:

◆ Life Coaching
◆ Career Coaching
◆ Executive Coaching
◆ Career Assessments
◆ Custom Resumes

Each of those might lead to another page that further elaborates on that particular service.

EXERCISE
Website Structure

1. **Explore the Web and find websites that you like, whose structure you can emulate.**

   These can be coaches' websites or those of other professionals or small businesses. List what you like (and don't like) about each website you review.

2. **Use the template on the following page to begin to structure your website. See the sample that follows for ideas.**

   On the top line, write your business or domain name.

   The second line is the navigation bar — the links that will take users to the main pages of your website.

   Below each entry on the Navigation Bar, write in the pages that users will access from that section. These can appear as a drop-down menu or as another menu that will appear once they get to that page.

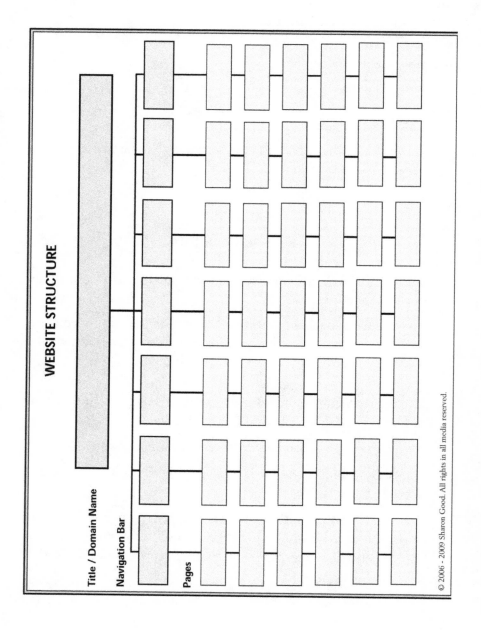

WEBSITE STRUCTURE

Title / Domain Name

Navigation Bar

Pages

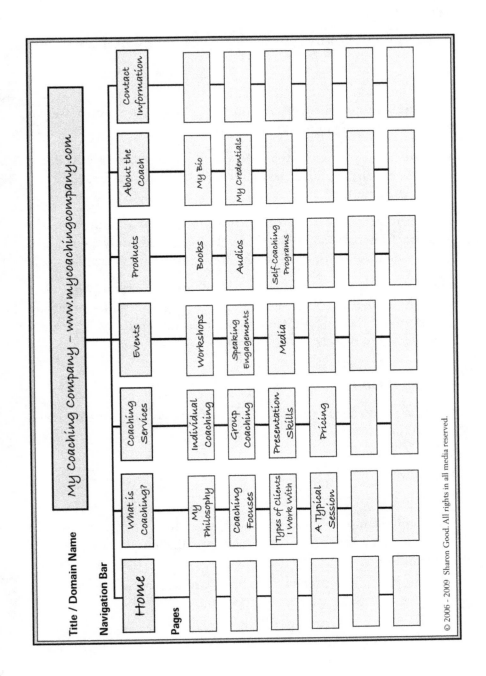

Web Design

Next, let's look at what goes into designing your website.

Some Guidelines

Whether you do your website yourself or work with a professional, keep the following in mind:

◆ Be sure that your website reflects the tone and professional image that you want to project, so that it "speaks" to your target audience. (Review chapter 3.)

◆ Keep it simple. Use an uncluttered background, and limit the number of colors and fonts that you use. Include only a few audio and video elements. Make it easy for users to find what they need.

◆ Make it consistent. Your design elements, navigation bars, colors and fonts should be the same on every page. Users like a uniform experience. Having a different setup or design on every page is confusing to them.

Getting It Done

There are three factors to consider in getting your website designed and produced:

◆ time
◆ money
◆ skill

If you have more time than money, you might want to consider a do-it-yourself website host. These sites provide templates, into which you can drop your text and graphics.

If you have more money than time, you probably want to hire a full-service Web designer to do it for you.

If you have good computer skills, it might be fun for you to either design a website from scratch or use a do-it-yourself host, where you can add your creative touch.

If you have "two left mice," you probably want to hire someone to do the whole job for you. If you can handle the page layout, but not the graphic design, you can hire someone to design the graphics (and possibly a page template), and then create the pages yourself, dropping in your text and graphics.

If you want to create your website yourself, the most popular Web design software is Adobe Dreamweaver. You can also design pages on other programs, such as Quark XPress and Microsoft Word, and convert them to HTML, although Dreamweaver gives you more control and flexibility. For graphics, check out Adobe Photoshop and Adobe Illustrator. For animation, you'll want Adobe Fireworks and Flash. To upload your files to your host's server, use an FTP program such as Fetch (for Mac) or Cuteftp.

If you choose to find a designer, get recommendations from friends and colleagues. If you come across a website you like, scroll down to the bottom of the page and see if there's a link to the Web designer, or query the owner of the website. You can also post your design job at sites such as Guru (www.guru.com) or Elance (www.elance.com) and select a designer who suits your style and budget.

Web Hosting

There are many options available for Web hosting. Most Web hosts offer a variety of hosting packages, with a wide array of features to suit both beginning and advanced users, at a range of prices. Most of them will also register your domain name as part of the package. (See chapter 3 for more on choosing your domain name.)

In choosing a Web host, consider the following options:

◆ Hosting packages and pricing options
◆ Full-service phone support vs. e-mail support only
◆ Availability of templates and site-builder tools for do-it-yourself website creation
◆ Availability of custom design and programming services
◆ Number of e-mail accounts

- Availability and number of autoresponders
- E-commerce and credit card processing
- Blogs
- Spam filters
- Newsletter broadcasting
- Numerous other advanced features

Also consider:
- How much Web space do you need?
- How many e-mail accounts do you need?
- Do you need to access your e-mail on the Web or only through the e-mail software on your computer?
- How much traffic to your website do you expect (i.e., how much bandwidth do you need)?
- Do you need to access visitor statistics?
- Will you be creating your own website (yourself or with a designer), or do you want do-it-yourself capability with templates?
- If you're doing it yourself, do you like the templates this host offers? How much flexibility is offered to customize your site?
- How reliable is their server? How quickly will pages load?
- How much support do they offer in creating your website? How easy is it to use?
- How good, and how responsive, is their technical support?

As you see, there are many variables in selecting a Web host. To make an informed choice, I suggest getting recommendations. Definitely check out their tech support services. Some of the do-it-yourself sites look easy at first glance, but once you get into the process, you may encounter problems that you can't resolve yourself.

Also, check with your Web designer to see if they offer hosting options (and how their prices compare to their competitors) or if they have providers that they prefer.

Your Internet service provider (ISP) may also offer you free Web space, but you might not be able to use your own domain name. You may have to use a Web address (URL) such as:

http://users.myisp.com/sharongood/goodlifecoaching.html

This makes it much harder for potential clients to find you. Also, keep in mind how you want to present yourself and your business — a convoluted Web address doesn't represent you well as a serious professional.

Maintaining Your Website

Once your website is up and running, it's important to keep it up-to-date. How professional does it look when your calendar lists workshops you did two years ago? You can easily learn to make simple updates yourself, or have your Web designer or assistant make changes for you.

Keep your links up-to-date as well. Broken links are not search-engine-friendly, and they make your website look like it's been abandoned.

Search engines also love new material, so make your website dynamic. Post articles, list new classes you're offering, or write a blog. Keep it fresh, and update it periodically to reflect how you and your coaching practice are evolving.

Making Your Website Search-Engine Friendly

Having a website doesn't mean people will automatically find you. You need to get potential clients to visit. Aside from putting your Web address on your e-mail signature, business card, brochure and other printed materials, you want people to be able to find you on the Web itself, usually through search engines.

Setting up your website to get the best possible ranking in the search engines is called **search engine optimization** (SEO). Any Web designer worth their salt should know how to optimize your website.

Here are some things you can contribute to the process yourself or make sure your designer is handling:

◆ Choose your domain name and keywords carefully. When people are looking for your services, what are some of the keywords they'll be searching?

◆ Use your important keywords in your page text, especially in the first paragraph. It's okay to use them a few times within a page, but don't overdo it. Search engines consider that "spamming," and it will actually *lower* your ranking.

◆ Have your Web designer include keywords, phrases and information in the page title, page description and metatags. The page title is visible in the top of the browser window. The page description and metatags (which include your keywords and other important information) are hidden within the page code, but are picked up by the "Web crawlers" that feed information to the search engines. The page description will show when your website comes up in a search, so use that as an opportunity to give a snapshot of who you are that will make readers want to learn more.

◆ Include "alternate text" (i.e., a label or description of the picture) for every graphic, and use Flash (animation) sparingly. Web crawlers can't read graphics, so beautiful though they may be, they don't help your ranking. Too many Flash files will slow down the rate at which your page loads, which can discourage some people from looking further at your site.

◆ Keep your data fresh. Add articles, events, blog entries, etc. Keep events calendars and hyperlinks updated. Outdated calendars look bad, and a load of broken hyperlinks will lower your ranking.

◆ Include links from your website to others, and get links from others to yours. You can do this by having a "resources" or "links" page and by trading listings with compatible websites. If you have an article published on another website, be sure to have them include your Web link. Make sure the links you include are relevant to your site content. Search engines are pretty savvy, and loading down your website with irrelevant links will lower your ranking.

◆ Register with the major search engines (Google, Yahoo, AltaVista, Lycos, Excite, Dogpile, etc.). You can use an inexpensive listing service, such as Site See (www.site-see.com), but be aware that you will get listed on hundreds of minor search engines along with the important ones (which will also result in a bunch of unwanted e-mails immediately after). It's best to register manually with the "big guys."

◆ To get premium placement, enroll in pay-per-click services, where you pay to get a better ranking when someone searches for your keywords. The two most popular services are:

    ◆ Google Adwords (adwords.google.com)
    ◆ Yahoo Search Marketing (searchmarketing.yahoo.com)

EXERCISE
Keywords

Make a list of keywords and phrases that your potential clients might use when searching for a coach. Start with the list you made in chapter 2 and see how many more you can come up with. Be sure to include the types of coaching you offer, as well as any other related services, and the types of clients you work with (e.g., artists, bankers, athletes, stay-at-home moms, etc.).

A Visual Summary

The illustration on the following page shows the flow of preparing a website, from defining your goals to your information reaching your potential customer.

1. **Define Goals**

   In this step, you determine your goals for your business, as well as what you want to accomplish with your website.

2. **Write Copy**

   Using your goals as your guideline, you write the copy for your Web pages, including your keywords in your copy.

3. **Design and Create Pages**

   Using your copy, you create a design for your website and produce all the pages.

4. **Optimize**

   You optimize your website by including your keywords in your copy, as well as in the page title and metatags. Notice how your page title shows up at the top of your Web browser page (A), and how the title and keywords appear in your hidden HTML code, or metatags (B).

5. **Upload Files**

   Your completed Web pages are uploaded to a Web host server. By using Internet search engines, which access your keywords, potential clients find you! Notice that the listing that comes up from the keyword search (C) matches the Meta Name description in the HTML code (B).

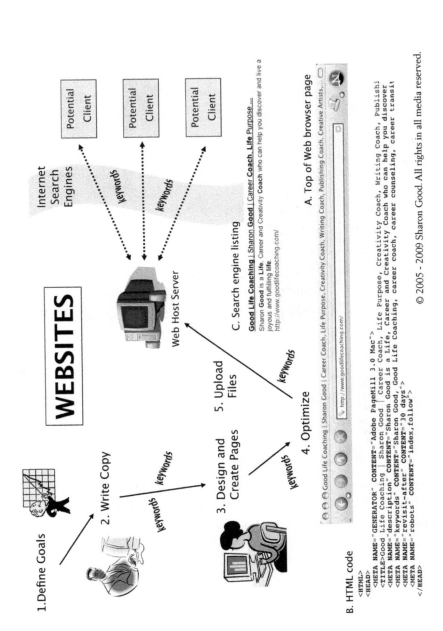

RESOURCES

The following resources are offered as suggestions, and NOT recommendations. Internet businesses in particular are notorious for changing. If you are considering using any of these vendors, check them out carefully and make an informed decision.

Books

Build Your Own Website The Right Way Using HTML & CSS, by Ian Lloyd

Create Your Own Website, by Scott Mitchell

Creating Web Sites: The Missing Manual, by Matthew MacDonald

Dreamweaver CS3: The Missing Manual, by David McFarland

How to Use the Internet to Advertise, Promote and Market Your Business or Website with Little or No Money, by Bruce C. Brown

Web Design and Marketing Solutions for Business Websites, by Kevin Potts

Website Optimization, by Andrew King

Website Hosting

Services for Coaches

Webvalence: www.webvalence.com

Webflexor Coaching: www.webflexor-coaching.com

Hosting for Coaching: www.hostingforcoaching.com

Coach Power Tools: www.coachpowertools.com

Do-It-Yourself / Low-Cost Websites, Domain Registration and Hosting

GoDaddy: www.godaddy.com

Homestead: www.homestead.com

Site Build It: buildit.sitesell.com

Yahoo Small Busines: smallbusiness.yahoo.com

Shopping Carts Plus: www.shoppingcartsplus.com

Web.com: www.web.com

Website for Free: www.websiteforfree.com

Doteasy: www.doteasy.com

Seanic: www.seanic.net

Register.com: www.register.com

000 Domains: www.000domains.com [those are zeros]

Domain.com: www.domain.com

Enom: www.enom.com

Who Is: www.whois.com

Search Engine Optimization, Site Submission

Self-Promotion: www.selfpromotion.com

Search Engine Watch: www.searchenginewatch.com

Yahoo Search: search.yahoo.com/info/submit.html

Google: www.google.com/services/

Add Me: www.addme.com

Site See Submission Service: www.site-see.com

Submit Express: www.submitexpress.com

Web, Graphics and Logo Designers

Guru: www.guru.com

Elance: www.elance.com

Coroflot: www.coroflot.com

Creative Hot List: www.creativehotlist.com

Web Software

Web Design and Maintenance

Adobe Dreamweaver: www.adobe.com/products/dreamweaver

Adobe Contribute: www.adobe.com/products/contribute

Graphic Design and Animation

Adobe Photoshop: www.adobe.com/products/photoshop

Adobe Illustrator: www.adobe.com/products/illustrator

Adobe Fireworks: www.adobe.com/products/fireworks

Adobe Flash: www.adobe.com/products/flash

As of the publication of this book, Adobe offers a package called Adobe Creative Suite 4 Web Premium that includes all of the above applications. For current information, visit: www.adobe.com/products/creativesuite/.

Royalty-Free Art

Artzooks: www.artzooks.com

Clipart.com: www.clipart.com

Getty Images: www.gettyimages.com

iStockphoto®: www.istockphoto.com

Do a search on "royalty-free art."

FTP *(File Transfer Protocol, for uploading files)*

CuteFTP: www.cuteftp.com/products/ftp_clients.aspx
SmartFTP: www.smartftp.com (PC only)
Fetch: www.fetchsoftworks.com (Mac only)

Information and Resources

Web Host for Life: www.webhostforlife.com
Web Monkey: www.webmonkey.com
Website Magazine: www.websitemagazine.com
Web Style Guide: www.webstyleguide.com

SIX

E-ZINES AND E-NEWSLETTERS

E-zines and e-newsletters are virtual magazines or newsletters (the terms are often used interchangeably). They may range from a full-blown, 8-page (or more) magazine to a monthly article to a weekly tip. They can be as simple or as complex as you want them to be.

For the sake of simplicity, I'll use the term "e-zine" throughout this chapter to refer to all types of e-zines and e-newsletters.

BENEFITS

◆ **Getting to know you**

E-zines give your audience an opportunity to experience you — what you have to offer, your philosophy, etc. — through regular exposure over time.

- **Regular contact / build a mailing list**

  E-zines provide you with a way to stay in touch with potential clients on a regular basis. By offering content that is of value to them, you're not just badgering them with sales materials. When they first meet you, they may not be ready to sign on for coaching. The more they see you—and get to know you—the more likely you'll be the first person to come to mind when they need your product or service.

- **Establish you as an expert**

  When you write about a subject on a regular basis, people begin to perceive you as an expert. This can help potential clients to trust you, as well as leading to media exposure.

- **Promote goodwill by sharing information and "free stuff"**

  With all of us being constantly bombarded by sales pitches, people appreciate receiving something of "added value" free of charge. Your e-zine gives you an opportunity to offer bits of interesting news and information that will be helpful to your target audience. You might also, from time to time, offer a free report or opportunity, such as an introductory session or free teleclass.

- **Keep clients informed of new classes, products, news, etc.**

  Some of your e-zine readers may never sign on for coaching, but they might be interested in classes or products you're offering. Keep them informed of new products, specials or discounts; let them know where you're doing classes or presentations; and share exciting successes (yours or your clients', with permission).

- **Extend your reach**

  E-zines take on a life of their own. They often get passed along to friends, and you can connect with more potential clients. I've had people contact me about coaching or show up in my classes because a friend forwarded my newsletter to them.

◆ **Leverage your articles**

The articles you write for your e-zine can be posted on your own website, complementary websites and sites that are specifically for posting articles (see chapter 9).

◆ **Develop your writing skills**

If you plan to use writing as a marketing tool, doing a regular e-zine is a great way to develop your skills: coming up with ideas, developing them into articles, meeting deadlines and refining your writing style.

GETTING STARTED

You have a lot of latitude in designing your e-zine. Like your website, you can use it to express your personality and your brand.

There are a few things you need to be aware of to get started.

Coordinate with Your Web Site

To support your brand, you'll coordinate the design elements, tone and content of your e-zine with those of your website (as well as your other materials).

- Your e-zine may have the same name and primary focus as your business and website. For example, if your business name is Get A Life Coaching, your e-zine might be called *Get A Life*. Your e-zine might also focus on a particular niche or target audience within your practice. For example, my website is Good Life Coaching, but my e-zine is *Living the Creative Life*, which points to my focus on creativity.

- You can archive articles from back issues on your website — this is a good way of updating your content and drawing people back to your website. You might post all of your back issues or a limited number. Alternatively, you can offer a back issue as a free giveaway to entice new subscribers.

Choose Your Format

There are several formats in which you can publish your e-zine.

◆ **HTML**

This is the most popular format. An HTML e-zine is sent in the body of an e-mail. It can be fully formatted, with columns, hyperlinks and graphics.

HTML e-zines are attractive and reinforce your visual brand identity. If you like statistics, some e-zine distribution hosts can track the percentage of list members that open and view your newsletter. On the down side, these are more likely to get blocked in SPAM filters (although there are workarounds available for this), and a few people are still using old browsers that don't read HTML.

◆ **PDF attachment**

An e-zine can be created in word processing or page layout software, fully formatted like a printed newsletter and converted to a PDF. The PDF is then attached to an e-mail, and the recipient downloads the file and opens it with Adobe Reader or Acrobat.

◆ **Plain text**

Plain text newsletters are the simplest to do. They are typed, using simple keyboard characters, into the body of an e-mail. They have little formatting and no graphics — although you can create some visual elements using keyboard characters, such as *=*=*=* or ^-^-^-^. They are not as visually pleasing as HTML, but they are easy to prepare and accessible on any e-mail software. (See appendix A for a sample plain-text newsletter.)

◆ **Link to a website**

Finally, you can create a simple e-mail that gives the first few sentences of each article and includes links to the full articles and features on your website. If you're doing a plain text e-zine, you can also add links in the e-mail to the fully-formatted articles on a

Web page, to give your readers the choice to read the plain-text version or the formatted Web version.

Publication Tips

Following are a few things to take into consideration as you plan your e-zine.

◆ Have a **clearly defined topic and title** that appeal to your target audience. Your e-zine may have the same name as your website and business name. If possible, include one or more of your keywords in your title.

◆ Use a **clear, consistent subject line** for the e-mail that contains your e-zine. People get a lot of e-mail these days, and if they don't recognize your e-zine from the subject line, they may just delete it. Some distribution systems put the title in [square brackets] to make it recognizable as an e-zine; you can also do that manually.

◆ Use the **same format** for each issue. Readers like predictability — imagine picking up your favorite magazine or newspaper and having a different format every time! Use the same masthead and include the same elements in each issue. So, if you have a feature article, a tip, a quote and information on new products or classes, do that for every issue, in the same order.

◆ Publish on **regular schedule**. People appreciate regularity, and it helps to keep you in their minds. The most common schedules are monthly, weekly and sometimes quarterly. The rule of thumb is, the more frequently you publish, the shorter the e-zine should be. So, a weekly e-zine might include a short essay or tip, while a monthly e-zine could include a full-length article.

Along with the results you want to produce, take into account how much time you want to spend on your e-zine. Hopefully, your business will be growing and you'll have less time to spend on your marketing tools.

Set it up for efficiency. Prepare in advance by jotting down ideas or even writing several articles at a time. For a tips e-zine, you might sit down and write out 52 weekly tips, then upload them to an autoresponder distribution system and forget about them for a year!

HOW TO WORK WITH E-ZINES

Content and Structure

Your e-zine can include a variety of content. The following components should *always* be included:

◆ **Masthead**

The masthead, which appears at the beginning of every e-zine, should include the title, issue/volume and date. You can also include a tag line and, if you're publishing in a graphic format, your logo and photo.

◆ **Disclaimer**

Because of the proliferation of SPAM, it's advisable to include a disclaimer, such as: "You are receiving this e-zine because you subscribed at MyWebsite.com. Your e-mail will not be shared with any third party."

◆ **Information about you and your coaching practice**

While an e-zine gives added value through articles, news and tips, you also want to remind readers about your coaching services. E-zines are often forwarded to friends, and your e-zine may fall into the Inbox of someone who doesn't know who you are.

◆ **Contact information**

Also because of SPAM, it's important to include a geographic location, so that readers know you're legitimate. This can be your office address or a post office box and can be included at the end of the e-zine.

◆ **How to subscribe / unsubscribe**

It's considered good manners to inform subscribers how to unsubscribe, should they no longer wish to receive your e-zine. Also, because people can easily forward your e-zine to friends, you want to let them know how they can subscribe if they want to receive your e-zine directly.

◆ **Copyright**

As with all digital copy, you want to include your copyright to discourage plagiarism. The notice may look like this:

© 2009 Sharon Good. All rights in all media reserved.

You can also choose from among the following components:

◆ **Table of contents**

If your e-zine is longer than a screen-length or two and contains several components, include a table of contents to let readers know what to expect in this issue.

◆ **Opening comments or personal note**

With longer e-zines, there's a trend nowadays to include a little personal opening piece. This may be about a trip you took, an experience you had or an event you attended. My preference is that the opening be relevant to the topic of the newsletter article, rather than a personal event. With graphical e-zines, you can also include a photo. While this is a great way to give clients an experience of you, keep it succinct and interesting.

◆ **Pictures / graphics / logo**

If your e-zine is in a graphical format, you can include a picture of yourself, your logo and attractive, relevant graphics to enhance the visual presentation.

◆ **Article**

This is the meat of your e-zine. The topic should be in line with the theme of your e-zine, and something that your target audience will want to read about. Remember that it's difficult to read on-screen, so make it long enough to give value, but not so long that people become fatigued before they can finish the article.

The placement of the article within the e-zine can vary. Some authors put the article after all their sales pitches. I prefer to have the article close to the top and the sales information later. To me, that demonstrates a generosity, rather than: Here's my sales pitch and, oh yeah, here's an article for you. Use your judgment about what feels right to you.

◆ **Tips or information**

You can offer a tip or information that's useful to your target audience. If you're doing a short, weekly e-zine, the tip itself may be the focus. For a longer e-zine, a tip can enhance or supplement the feature article.

◆ **Quotes / book lists / resources**

You can include various resources that enhance your feature article. These may be relevant quotes, books, Web links, etc.

◆ **News**

Let your readers know if you have been or will be featured in the media or will be speaking somewhere. You can also share other news about yourself or your business, or anything relevant to the interests and concerns of your target audience.

◆ **The sales pitch**

Let readers know about your books, e-books, audios, videos, workshops and programs. Include a short blurb, along with a link to more information on your website, or to an e-commerce site where they can purchase those products or services. In an HTML e-zine, the sales pitch may be placed in a column parallel to your feature article.

◆ **Testimonials or success stories**

You can include one or two short testimonials or client success stories to support the information on your coaching services. Potential clients feel more comfortable approaching you when they see that you've been successful with other clients.

◆ **Offer something for free**

People love getting free gifts. You might run a contest, offer a free report or e-booklet or give a time-limited discount on a product or service.

EXERCISE
E-zine Components and Structure

Select the different components that you would like to include in your e-zine. Number them in the order in which they will appear.

	Order
✔ Masthead	_____
✔ Disclaimer	_____
✔ Information about my coaching practice	_____
✔ Contact information	_____
✔ How to subscribe / unsubscribe	_____
✔ Copyright	_____
❑ Table of contents	_____
❑ Opening comments or personal note	_____
❑ Article	_____
❑ My picture	_____

	Order
❏ Pictures / graphics / logo	_____
❏ Tips or information	_____
❏ Quotes / book lists / resources	_____
❏ News	_____
❏ Sales pitch	_____
❏ Testimonials or success stories	_____
❏ A freebie or giveaway	_____
❏ _____	_____
❏ _____	_____
❏ _____	_____

Ideas for Creating Content

In creating an e-zine on a regular basis, you may fear that you will run out of ideas. Here are a few to prime the pump:

◆ Address common questions and concerns that your target audience has. If you're not sure what those are, ask them!

◆ Look for interesting, relevant books and use them as the basis for an article.

◆ Invite guest writers or do interviews.

◆ Put out a question to your readers on a topic of interest to your audience, and publish or write about their responses.

◆ Do some keyword searches on the Internet and look for timely topics.

Keep an idea file, so that when it's time to write a new issue, you'll have a stash of possibilities from which you can draw.

Managing Content

Managing content for an e-zine is similar to managing website content. People are reading off the screen, so the same rules apply (see chapter 5).

Here are some additional tips:

◆ Most people write their own e-zine. You want the personal touch, and it's hard (although not impossible) to find someone who can write in your style. If you're not great with spelling and grammar, do have someone edit your copy.

◆ Keep it succinct. Remember — on the Web, less is more. The general rule is to write about half of what you'd write for a printed article. And be sure to make your copy catchy and enticing.

◆ Break the text into chunks. It's hard to read big blocks of text on the screen. Paragraphs should be two to four sentences long.

◆ Use sub-headings — one to three words that quickly and easily describe what's coming.

◆ For lists, use bullet points to set them off.

◆ After your e-zine is published, post the articles on your website to keep it dynamic. You can also look for other related websites that need content, as well as article and e-zine distribution sites.

EXERCISE
Writing Your E-zine

Using the components you selected in the previous exercise, write a draft of your e-zine. You may want to try the components in different orders to see which you like best.

Once your format is set, write several issues to help you "get in the groove," especially if your format is short. Use the sample in Appendix A as a model, or refer to the e-zines you subscribe to for inspiration.

❧

Designing Your E-Zine

The way you design your e-zine depends on which format you use.

♦ For an HTML e-zine, you'll want to coordinate the design with that of your website, to reinforce your brand. Have your Web designer lay out a template for your e-zine. You may want to have that person do the layout for each issue or teach you how to do it. With HTML, you can also include graphics.

♦ For a PDF e-zine, you'll lay it out in a word processor or page layout software and convert it to a PDF. You may want to use Adobe Acrobat to add enhancements such as bookmarks or hyperlinks.

♦ With a plain text e-zine, you're limited to the characters you see on your keyboard. For mastheads and borders, you can create simple designs using keyboard characters, such as:

^^^^^^^^^^^^^^^^^^^^^^^

MY FABULOUS E-ZINE

<><><><><><><><><><>

Use ALL CAPS for titles and asterisks (*) or dashes (--) for bullets.

♦ You can also set up your e-zine as a page on your website and send subscribers the link.

Once you've designed your layout, test it on different e-mail programs. You might send your sample to a few friends and see how it appears on their system.

Distributing Your E-Zine

Now that you've put together your e-zine, you need to sign up subscribers and get the e-zine out to them. Some methods are simple, but labor-intensive. Others are automated and allow your list to grow without any additional work for you.

Here are some of the ways you can distribute an e-zine:

◆ **Your own e-mail program**

When your list is small, you can create an e-mail group and broadcast your e-zine from Outlook or Thunderbird or whichever e-mail program you use. This is fine when your subscriber list is small, but it becomes unwieldy when it grows. Since it requires you to subscribe people manually, it's more work for you.

◆ **List management software**

You can purchase software that allows you to manage subscribers and automates many of the processes. This is most useful if you have a large subscriber database and want to keep it in-house.

◆ **Free or paid list hosts**

These websites manage and store your subscriber lists and allow you to broadcast your e-zine to your entire list with one e-mail. They include an "opt-in" feature, which prevents someone from subscribing people to your e-zine without their permission — an e-mail is sent to the subscriber to confirm or "opt in." If they don't respond, it means that they decline the subscription.

If your subscriber list is fairly small, you can use a free service such as Topica or Yahoo Groups. More extensive lists, or more frequent mailings, will require a paid service such as Constant Contact, which also offers more sophisticated features.

Hosting your e-zine through websites such as Topica and Yahoo Groups can also attract new subscribers to your list through category and keyword searches made by visitors to those sites. You can also use these services to set up a public chat group around your topic without installing software on your own website.

If you plan to grow your list, using a host right from the start is your best option. See the Resources section of this chapter for additional hosting services.

Newsletter Etiquette

If you want people to subscribe to your e-zine — and stay subscribed — there are some rules of etiquette that are de rigueur.

It is *vitally important* to keep your e-mail list private, so that your subscribers are not inundated with SPAM. Some ways to do that:

◆ Never sell or give away access to your mailing list — to anyone!

◆ If you're using a list host to distribute your e-zine, be sure to set it to "announcement only," so that no one but you can send e-mails to your list. (If you use a list host as a chat group, then you can set it to "open discussion" — but that should be a separate list.)

◆ If you're distributing from your own computer, make sure each person you send the e-mail to is designated as "bcc" (which stands for "blind carbon copy"). This means that no one else on the list will get their e-mail address.

◆ If you're going to use your e-zine to promote someone else's products, keep it to a minimum. Unless your offerings are highly appealing to your readers, they'll quickly unsubscribe if your e-zine becomes one big sales pitch.

Also note that e-zines are generally distributed for free. While they do not make money for you directly, they cost little or nothing to create and distribute, and they can bring people to your website and lead to sales of your products or services.

If you do want to create a paid e-zine, it needs to be a serious enterprise that provides information that is hard to find elsewhere and worth paying for on a regular basis.

Promoting Your E-Zine

Like your website, your e-zine is not a "build it and they will come" situation. You need to promote it. Some ways to do that:

- Mention it on your printed materials (business card, brochure, etc.).

- Include a teaser in your e-mail signature (e.g., "<u>Click here</u> to sign up for my free e-zine, *Life is Good*").

- List it with online e-zine directories, and also have your articles published on other websites (see Resources).

- When someone arrives at your website, have a very visible link that leads to a sign-up form, or have a pop-up window that comes up as soon as someone arrives at your home page.

- Send a sample issue on request, or archive past issues on your website.

- Sign people up at speaking engagements and workshops.

- Offer an incentive for signing up, such as an e-booklet or special report (see chapter 10).

When an e-zine is well-done and well-promoted, it's an easy and inexpensive way to demonstrate your expertise and connect with your target audience on a regular basis, and a great way to develop your writing ability.

RESOURCES

The following resources are offered as suggestions, and NOT recommendations. Internet businesses in particular are notorious for changing. If you are considering using any of these vendors, check them out carefully and make an informed decision.

Hosting / Distribution

1 Shopping Cart: www.1shoppingcart.com
Aweber Communications: www.aweber.com
Constant Contact: www.constantcontact.com
Emma: www.myemma.com
EZ Ezine: www.ezezine.com
List Rocket: www.listrocket.com
Sparklist: www.sparklist.com
Topica: www.topica.com
Yahoo Groups: groups.yahoo.com
Webvalence: www.webvalence.com

Books

E-newsletters That Work: The Small Business Owner's Guide To Creating, Writing and Managing An Effective Electronic Newsletter, by Michael J. Katz
Extraordinary Blogs And Ezines, by Lynne Rominger

Expert Advice

Email Universe: Email Newsletter Publishing Strategies: www.emailuniverse.com

E-zine Directories

Go-Ezines: www.go-ezines.com
My Favorite Ezines: www.myfavoriteezines.com
The Ezine Directory: www.ezine-dir.com
Web Source: www.web-source.net/web/Ezines/
Zinester: subs.zinester.com

 **SEVEN**

BLOGS

Blogs—short for "weblogs"—are basically online journals. They're kind of a cross between a newsletter and a chat room. Some are simply commentaries from the author, while others allow and encourage replies and interaction.

Blogs were initially popular with younger people, but they're quickly catching on with all ages as a great way to share information, keep yourself "out there" and connect with your target audience.

BENEFITS

◆ **Communicate instantly**

With an e-zine, you have to wait until your publication date to communicate a new idea to your audience. With a blog, you can add an entry on the spot, which allows it to be current and immediate.

◆ **Easy to use**

With blogging hosts, you just have to open an account, set your preferences and go. Many Web hosts also offer blogging as an optional feature.

◆ **Chatty and personal**

While e-zines tend to be more formally written, like a magazine article, blogs are more informal, like a journal entry. It's a great way to give people a personal experience of you.

◆ **Share useful information**

A blog is a great way to share timely news and useful resources with your audience and offer added value. One caveat: Make it professionally relevant. Personally, I would not be interested in reading extended treatises on someone's pets, kids or vacations — unless, of course, it was related to the focus of their business!

◆ **Search-engine friendly**

Because blogs are updated often, they put you in a good position with search engines, which thrive on new content.

◆ **Interactivity**

If you'd like, you can make your blog interactive by allowing readers to respond to your posts. This attracts people who like to dialogue, and it's a great way to keep them coming back. You can use it to "feel out" your target audience and get feedback on issues related to your business.

◆ **A good way to practice writing**

If writing is a part of your marketing strategy, a blog is a great way to polish your written expression and practice on a regular basis.

◆ **An inexpensive Web presence**

If your needs are simple and you present yourself professionally, a blog can be a simple, low-cost, entry-level website. In fact, most blogs are free. They just require an investment of your time.

Blogs vs. E-zines

Blogs and e-zines may both have a place in your marketing strategy, or you may choose one over the other. Here are some of the ways they compare.

BLOG	E-ZINE
Short, chatty, conversational	More formal and structured
Publish whenever you want — communicate timely information instantly	Publish on regular schedule
Reader has to come to you*	Shows up in reader's mailbox
Can be interactive	One-way communication
Read online	Can be forwarded
Show your personality while sharing knowledge	Share your knowledge while showing your writing ability

* Most blogs now offer a way for fans to be notified when a new entry is posted.

EXERCISE
Blog or E-zine?

If you're deciding between doing a blog or an e-zine, make a list of the pros and cons of each. Read through this chapter and chapter 6 for ideas.

GETTING STARTED

Before you get started, keep in mind that a blog is a commitment. If you start a blog, you need to add entries on a regular basis — a minimum of two to three times a week. If you stop writing for a period of time, you'll lose momentum and lose your audience.

Setting Goals for Your Blog

Similar to setting up a website, begin by determining your goals for your blog. Do you want to:

◆ **Express yourself through writing**

If you love to write and share information, a blog is a great opportunity to write on a regular basis and know you're connecting with a receptive audience.

◆ **Attract an audience for your coaching business**

With a blog, you can show your personality, share your views and philosophy and attract clients who resonate with you.

◆ **Engage your audience in a dialogue**

You can give potential clients an opportunity to comment on your blog entries. It's a great way to learn what their concerns are.

◆ **Be a resource and provide tips and information**

People love getting something for free. In your blog, you can share tips and information that will be of interest to your target audience.

◆ **Connect with your audience in a spontaneous and timely way**

While a website is fairly "set" and an e-zine comes out on a regular schedule, with a blog, you can post an entry any time you want. This is a great way of connecting, particularly with people who love the Web and enjoy checking your blog for new entries — sometimes several times a day. When they're thinking about finding a coach, you'll be at the top of their list.

EXERCISE
Goals For My Blog

Check off your goals for your blog. Add any that are not on the list.

❑ Express myself through writing

❑ Attract an audience for my coaching business

❑ Dialogue with my audience and learn more about their concerns

❑ Be a resource and share information

❑ Connect with my audience in a spontaneous way

❑ _____

❑ _____

❑ _____

✁

HOW TO WORK WITH BLOGS

Setting Up Your Blog

Setting up a blog is pretty easy. Generally, your hosting service will lead you through the process.

◆ **Choose a blogging host**

Blog hosting is usually free. Try one of the hosts listed in the Resources for this chapter, do an Internet search on "blog hosts," or ask your friends for recommendations. Some Web hosts also include blogging as an option. Compare several that look good to you and select one.

◆ **Create an account**

Follow the directions to set up an account with your host service.

◆ **Choose a name for your blog**

As with an e-zine, it's wise to coordinate the name of your blog with your website and business name.

◆ **Select categories and tags**

Similar to keywords, these help interested readers find you.

◆ **Choose a template**

If possible, coordinate the look and colors with those of your website, and include your business logo and your picture.

◆ **Choose whether to allow Comments (interactivity)**

Think about whether you want readers to participate, or whether you want to keep posting rights for yourself.

◆ **Write your first message**

Post an introductory greeting, welcoming readers and giving an idea of what you'll be writing about. Then, keep writing on a regular basis!

◆ **Link to your website**

If you have a website, set up a link to your blog. If not, use your blog as your Web presence. You can also add the link to your LinkedIn or Facebook profile (see chapter 15).

◆ **Make sure you have a "presence"**

All too often, I come across a wonderful blog that gives absolutely no indication of who is writing the blog and how I can reach them. As a marketing tool, this is a waste of your time and effort. You want potential clients to be able to find you! Make sure you include your name, business name and e-mail and/or Web address.

Working Your Blog

Now that your blog is up and running, you need to get people there and keep it alive and dynamic.

◆ **Advertise the URL (web address) on your printed and digital materials**

While some people may find your blog through keyword searches, you need to direct people there as well. Include the URL on your business card, brochure, website, e-mail signature and any other materials you send out to the public. If you appear in the media (see chapter 14), mention the URL to your audience.

◆ **Add entries regularly**

Once you've started your blog, you need to write on a regular basis. Get your readers in the habit of checking back frequently to see what fabulous information you've added.

◆ **Keep it relevant**

Make sure the content is of interest to your target audience. As a multifaceted person, you have many things you can write about. To make the blog an effective marketing tool, the content needs to matter to the people you want to attract into your coaching practice. If you want to write about personal matters, have a completely separate blog or website.

◆ **Keep it interesting and valuable**

Find things to write about that will keep your audience interested and make it worth their while to take time out of their day to visit your blog. If you want to write about the adorable things your dog did or the fantastic cruise you took, find a way to link it back to topics that are important to your target audience.

◆ **Use your keywords**

As with all Web-based outlets, you want to include your keywords in your text to help people find you through the search engines. Refer to the list of keywords you created in chapter 5.

Using a Blog as Your Website

When you're beginning your coaching practice, especially if you're on a budget, you can use a one-page blog to establish your Web presence. With just a single page, you want to keep your text succinct and to the point. Include at least the following components:

- Your name

- Your business name (if you've chosen one)

- Your location — for safety, you might not want to include a street address, but do include your city

- A description of coaching

- Your niches and services, and how you help clients

- A short bio and possibly your photo

- Contact information

Keep in mind that with a blog, you can't use your own domain name (you can include your name as *part* of the URL), so this is a temporary solution. Eventually, you'll want your own identity, and you'll need to include many more pages and components than a blog allows.

As your business grows, refer to chapter 5 to set up a full-blown website with room for all the components you want to include and more extensive text.

RESOURCES

The following resources are offered as suggestions, and NOT recommendations. Internet businesses in particular are notorious for changing. If you are considering using any of these vendors, check them out carefully and make an informed decision.

Blogging Hosts

Blogger: www.blogger.com
BlogHarbor: www.blogharbor.com
EasyJournal: www.easyjournal.com
LiveJournal: www.livejournal.com
Movable Type: www.movabletype.com
TypePad: www.typepad.com
WordPress: www.wordpress.com
Xanga: www.xanga.com

Books

Blog Marketing, by Jeremy Wright
Blogging: Genius Strategies for Instant Web Content, by Biz Stone
Buzz Marketing with Blogs for Dummies, by Susannah Gardner
Extraordinary Blogs and Ezines, by Lynne Rominger
The Rough Guide to Blogging, by Jonathan Yang
The Weblog Handbook: Practical Advice on Creating and Maintaining Your Blog, by Rebecca Blood

Blog Search Engines

Blog Search dot com: www.blogsearch.com
Blog Search.com: www.blog-search.com
Blog Search Engine: www.blogsearchengine.com
Technorati: www.technorati.com

EIGHT

PODCASTS

Podcasts are radio shows that you can listen to online or download to your computer and mp3 player. They can be as short as a few minutes or as long as an hour or two.

Podcasts have become a popular way to carry your favorite radio shows with you when you leave the house, via an iPod or other mp3 player. If you enjoy being a "radio personality," podcasts can be a great way to connect with potential clients.

BENEFITS

Podcasts have similar benefits to e-zines.

◆ **A personal, "live" experience of you**

Remember, clients hire you because of a personal connection. Hearing your voice brings it one step closer than the written word.

◆ **Demonstrate your expertise**

Clients hire you because you have expertise they can benefit from. What better way to demonstrate that expertise than by talking about it on a radio show? You can share useful information and tips for your target audience, as well as demonstrating your coaching ability with call-ins or invited guests.

◆ **Reach people on a regular basis**

Like an e-zine, your audience receives your podcast on a regular basis, so your name stays in front of them.

◆ **Express your inner speaker / performer**

If there's a ham in you that needs to get out, a podcast is the perfect outlet. You can design a format that shows off your talents to best advantage and gives you the opportunity to strut your stuff.

◆ **Stay in touch**

If you do your radio show live, you can invite people to call in and ask questions about your area of expertise. Even if your show is prerecorded, you can bring a guest into your studio; invite listeners to contact you by e-mail, and then comment during your show; or even choose show topics based on their requests.

◆ **Convenience and portability**

Nowadays, people love "on demand" media. A podcast can be downloaded to a computer or mp3 player and played back anytime, anywhere.

GETTING STARTED

Exploring Podcasts

In beginning with podcasts, it would be useful to see what's already out there.

You'll need software to "catch" your podcasts. For simplicity, let's work with Apple's iTunes, which is available for both Mac and PC. If it's not already loaded on your computer, you can download it for free at www.apple.com/ipod/start.

Once you have the software installed, launch the application. Click on "iTunes Store" in the list on the left. Once the store window loads, click on Podcasts in the left column of that window.

Finally, under Quick Links in the right column, click on "Power Search." Now, do some keyword searches to find podcasts in your niche, such as "life coach," "career coach," "executive coach," etc. You'll be amazed at the list that comes up!

As you're listening to some of these examples, listen for:

♦ **Content**

What subjects are they talking about? What "segments" do they include? Do they do the show alone or bring on guests? How do they promote themselves as coaches? What do you like and dislike about the way they do that?

♦ **Tone**

What's the feeling of the podcast? Is it business-like? Friendly? Touchy-feely? What does the opening music lead you to expect?

♦ **How people are presenting themselves**

What's your impression of the host? What are they projecting? Are they presenting themselves well? What do you like about their presentation? What would you do differently?

♦ **Anything else you notice**

EXERCISE
Exploring Podcasts

Using the process just above, explore various podcasts in your niche. Keep notes about what you notice. Include what you like, what you don't like and what you want to include in your own podcast. Make a note of skills and content that you would like to develop.

Listening to Podcasts

Most often, when people find podcasts they like, they subscribe. Then, each time they launch iTunes (or another "podcatcher"), it automatically updates all of their subscriptions. When they connect their iPod (or another mp3 player) to their computer, the podcasts that they've selected to transfer also automatically update. Then, they can listen either on their computer or their mp3 player.

Supporting Your Brand

It's important to create a consistent image across all of your marketing tools. As with your website and e-zine, your podcast should reflect your "brand."

Choose a topic that coordinates with your Web presence and that will attract the type of clients you want. For example, if you want clients who are young business professionals or spiritual seekers or working moms, create a show that appeals to their tastes and addresses topics of interest to them.

Make sure the tone, including the opening music you use, is appropriate for your audience. Using New Age-y music will undercut your credibility if you're focusing on business professionals (even if they like it in their off hours!).

Terminology

Podcasting is very technical, and there are many technical terms you'll come across. Following are just a few that can be helpful to know:

mp3 — a kind of compressed audio file that is used for podcasting.

RSS Feed — Really Simple Syndication, the most popular news feed syndication format. RSS is used to provide items containing short descriptions of Web content together with a link to the full version of the content. This information is delivered as an XML file called an RSS feed, RSS stream, or RSS channel. Users can subscribe to an RSS feed to be notified when a new podcast is available.

Podcast — an RSS feed containing audio.

Show — the ongoing title of your show, such as "The Good Life! with Sharon Good."

Episode — an individual broadcast of your show.

Aggregator — a program used to collect and read RSS feeds. Also known as a newsreader, news aggregator or RSS aggregator. Readers may exist as stand-alone programs; operate as extensions of Web browsers or e-mail programs; or they may be available online.

Distributor — a website where you can subscribe to podcasts.

Host — a website whose server will hold and maintain your podcast files.

Podcatcher — a program that automatically detects and downloads podcasts that you've subscribed to.

ID3 Tag — an addition to mp3 files that allows data such as the file's title, performer, category and even cover art to be stored directly in the file.

Ping service — these services update different search engines, notifying them that a new podcast is available.

HOW TO WORK WITH PODCASTS

Podcasts are one of the more technical of our tools. Fortunately, over the last couple of years, many services, tools and packages have been developed to support you through the production process. Since the purpose of this book is to provide an overview, you can refer to the tools in the Resource section or search the Web for more extensive support when you're ready to go into production.

As always, we begin with planning.

Content

◆ **Topic and title**

Choose a topic and title that coordinate with your Website and e-zine. These, of course, will appeal to your target audience.

◆ **Format**

Select a format for your show. As with e-zines, it's best to have a consistent format, so your listeners know what to expect. Radio shows are often broken into "segments." Some of the segments you might use include:

- setting the agenda—what you'll be covering in this episode
- relevant information
- guest interviews
- coaching demonstrations
- news and tips
- book reviews
- updates on your coaching programs, public appearances, workshops, products, special offers, etc.

Use your podcast to demonstrate your expertise and skill. Share knowledge, give examples (protecting clients' identities, of course) and, if you choose, demonstrate coaching with guests or call-ins. This is also an opportunity to promote your coaching services, products and workshops.

You also need to decide on the length and frequency of your show. Your podcast may be as short as five to ten minutes or as long as an hour or more. You want to make it accessible to your audience, who are most likely busy people, so avoid going much more than an hour.

Plan to broadcast on a regular basis. Short podcasts might be broadcasted every day or two, while a longer show could be aired weekly or biweekly. When planning, take into account how much time you are willing and able to spend on production.

◆ **Music and tag line**

Having an opening theme is a great way to get your listeners "prepped" for your podcast. Keep it short. Anything more than 10 to 15 seconds seems very long when you're waiting for the content to begin. You may also want to have a recognizable tag line, such as, "This is Mary Jones, and I'm here to coach you!" You can also use the same music to end your show.

◆ **Plan each episode**

Think ahead and plan a list of varied topics to use for your shows. Write scripts or outlines. In the beginning, you may want to have it written out in more detail, but be careful of sounding like you're reading. Outlines or bullet points are best. Have "optional" material available, so you can be flexible if your podcast is running short or going overtime.

EXERCISE
Create Content for Your Podcast

Using the process just above, begin to create the format and content for your podcast.

Production

Now that you've got your content planned, let's get to work putting together your podcast.

◆ **Rehearse**

Try out your script, so that you can get comfortable with it. Record your rehearsals, so you can hear how you're sounding and note any changes you might want to make. Time each segment, so you get a feel for how long it takes.

As a new podcaster, you might find it useful to get feedback from an experienced radio person or trusted colleagues, or to seek out media training.

◆ Record

If you have the financial resources, you will get the best sound quality in a professional recording studio. But home equipment has come a long way, and it's easy to get a good-sounding recording from home, without spending a lot of money.

Find a quiet place, free of distraction. (If you want to simulate the sound of a recording booth, go into your closet!) Listen carefully for any humming or atmospheric noises. If you live in a noisy area, close the windows and turn off fans, air conditioning, phones, etc.

Digital recording is best, so you don't have to convert from a tape. You can record onto your computer, to an mp3 player or PDA with recording capability, or use a Web-based service such as Audio Acrobat.

If you're recording by phone and want to bring in a guest, you can use Audio Acrobat along with three-way calling. Many conferencing services, such as FreeConferenceCall® (www.freeconferencecall.com) offer a recording option, but test it out to make sure you're happy with the quality of the sound.

If you record directly onto your computer, you'll need audio software, such as Audacity or Audio Hijack (see Resources for more ideas). You'll also need a decent-quality microphone. If you're in a noisy location, opt for a headset microphone with noise canceling. Be sure to test it out. See how close you need to be to get the best possible sound quality. You might want to add a "pop filter" if your p's and t's are causing a puff or clicking sound.

In the beginning, you may want to do two or three "takes" of your segments, until you get in the groove with your recording technique and radio personality. You might even record a few shows for practice, without putting them "on the air."

◆ **Edit**

Once your show is recorded, you may want to edit the content (see Resources for software suggestions). You can take out parts you're not happy with or cut it to fit your time slot, as well as adding opening and closing music and an opening tag line. If your audio file is not already in mp3 format, you'll need to convert it.

EXERCISE
Record Your Podcast

Using the process just above, record and edit one or more podcasts.

Distribution

Now that you've got some shows, you'll need to get them to your audience.

◆ **Find a hosting service**

You'll need a hosting service where you can store your audio files and their supporting materials. Some services are free, others charge a fee. See the Resources section of this chapter for a few suggestions, or do a Web search on "podcast host."

In choosing a host, some of the criteria you'll need to look for are:

- reliability
- the amount of storage space available
- additional services, such as auto-pinging

◆ **Prepare supporting materials**

Each podcast requires "show notes" — a brief description of the content of each show. Show notes let listeners know what each show is about and help attract new listeners. They can be in paragraph or outline form and may include images. Your notes may include:

- A specific, captivating title to attract listeners
- The podcaster's name: you!
- A description of the show
- A few keywords relevant to the show's theme and content
- The category in which you want your podcast to be listed
- Links to resources that you mention in the show
- A link to download the mp3 directly
- A small logo or image that looks good at 50 x 50 pixels

Some podcasting hosts also include blogs for promoting your podcast, or you may want to set up your own. (See chapter 7 on Blogs.)

◆ Upload

Once your podcast is recorded and edited and your supporting materials written, you'll upload it to your hosting service. If your host doesn't provide a way to do that, or if your file is too big, you can use FTP software, such as Smart FTP or Fetch, to upload your audio file.

◆ Promote

A podcast doesn't do any good unless someone is listening. Promote your podcast as you would an e-zine: Include it in your e-mail signature, on your business card and on other virtual and printed materials.

To stimulate interest and discussion and connect listeners, you can use an interactive blog, or set up a chat room on your website or through a service such as Topica (www.topica.com) or Yahoo Groups (groups.yahoo.com).

EXERCISE
Get Your Podcast Out to Your Public

Using the process just above, find a podcasting host, upload your materials and start promoting!

❦

RESOURCES

The following resources are offered as suggestions, and NOT recommendations. Internet businesses in particular are notorious for changing. If you are considering using any of these vendors, check them out carefully and make an informed decision.

Podcasting Tutorials and Tools

About.com Radio:
　　radio.about.com/od/podcastin1/a/aa030805a.htm
Apple / iTunes:
　　www.apple.com/itunes/store/podcaststechspecs.html
Audacity: audacityteam.org/wiki/index.php?title=Creating_a_
　　simple_voice_and_music_Podcast_with_Audacity
How Stuff Works: www.howstuffworks.com/podcasting.htm
How to Podcast Tutorials:
　　◆ www.how-to-podcast-tutorial.com/00-podcast-tutorial-four-
　　　ps.htm
　　◆ www.how-to-podcast-tutorial.com/17-audacity-tutorial.htm
Podcasting Tools: www.podcasting-tools.com/how-to-podcast.htm

Books

The Business Podcasting Book: Launching, Marketing, and Measuring Your Podcast, by Greg Cangialosi, et al

How to Do Everything with Podcasting, by Shel Holtz with Neville Hobson

Podcasting Bible, by Mitch Ratcliffe and Steve Mack

Podcasting for Profit: A Proven 7-Step Plan to Help Individuals and Businesses Generate Income Through Audio and Video Podcasting, by Leesa Barnes

Podcast Solutions: The Complete Guide to Audio and Video Podcasting, by Michael Geoghegan and Dan Klass

Promoting Your Podcast: The Ultimate Guide to Building an Audience of Raving Fans, by Jason Van Orden

Secrets of Podcasting: Audio Blogging for the Masses, by Bart G. Farkas

Web-based Recording Services

Audio Acrobat: www.audioacrobat.com

Free Conference®: www.freeconference.com

Free Conference Call®: www.freeconferencecall.com

Podblaze: www.podblaze.com

Hardware

Podcasting kits (microphones, mixers, etc): www.macmall.com or www.pcmall.com, search "podcasting"

BSW Professional Audio Gear: www.bswusa.com/podcast.asp

Microphones: some suggested brands (some with headsets):
- – Altec Lansing
- – Labtech
- – Logitech
- – Plantronics

Software

Adobe Audition (formerly Cool Edit Pro):
www.adobe.com/products/audition/

Audacity and LAME: audacity.sourceforge.net

GarageBand (part of Apple's iLife):
www.apple.com/ilife/garageband/

Audio Hijack: www.rogueamoeba.com/audiohijack/

Fission: www.rogueamoeba.com/fission/

See also Additional Resources below and Resources, chapter 11.

Distribution / Directories / Aggregators

Feedburner: feedburner.google.com

iTunes: www.apple.com/itunes/

Odeo: www.odeo.com

Podbean: www.podbean.com

Podcast.com: podcast.com

Podcast Alley: www.podcastalley.com

Podnova: www.podnova.com

Hosting Services

Blog Talk Radio: www.blogtalkradio.com

Podbean: www.podbean.com

Podcast Revolution: www.podcastrevolution.com

Podhoster: www.podhoster.com

See also Additional Resources below.

Ping Services

Autopinger: autopinger.com
Kloth: www.kloth.net/services/ping.php
Ping-o-matic: pingomatic.com

Royalty-Free Music and Sound Effects

The Beat Suite: www.beatsuite.com
Free Play Music: freeplaymusic.com
Partners in Rhyme: www.partnersinrhyme.com
Royalty Free Music: www.royaltyfreemusic.com
Shockwave-Sound: www.shockwave-sound.com
Unique Tracks: www.uniquetracks.com

Podcatchers *(for listening to podcasts)*

iTunes: www.apple.com/itunes/download/
Juice: juicereceiver.sourceforge.net
An mp3 player

Additional Resources

Podcasting Tools: www.podcasting-tools.com

 **NINE**

ARTICLES

If you like to write, articles are a great way to get your name and your message out to potential clients. Articles can be published both in print and on the Web.

BENEFITS

◆ **Establish yourself as an expert**

People are impressed when they see something in print. When you have an article published in a magazine or newspaper, or even on the Web, you become a trusted expert on your topic.

◆ **Get your message out**

Many of us become coaches because we want to make positive changes in the world and help people. Articles are a great way to share your philosophy and let people know what you're passionate about — which often coincides with your coaching focus! Potential clients will relate to your message, and you'll be at the top of their list when they consider hiring a coach.

◆ **Credibility with clients**

Getting published gives you credibility. While people know that you paid for an advertisement, being accepted for publication is like getting an endorsement from the powers that be. It helps potential clients to feel comfortable that you know what you're doing as a coach.

◆ **Name recognition**

The coaching field (as with many businesses) has become a PR game. People like to buy from a familiar name. Publishing a series of articles or books (see chapter 10) will increase your name recognition, as well as enhancing the search engine ranking of your website. Clients looking for a coach may track you down after seeing your name in print.

◆ **Ability to target your efforts**

When pursuing placement for your articles, you can choose publications (magazines, newspapers, newsletters, websites) that will be read by the particular audience that you want to attract.

◆ **Multiple uses**

Once you write an article, it can be used over and over again. Unless the original publication holds the copyright, you can shop your articles around, perhaps tweaking them for particular publications. You can also post articles on your website and other complementary sites on the Internet. You might even compile a series of related articles into a book.

GETTING STARTED

By now, you know that I'm going to say that your articles should coordinate with and support your "brand." As a multifaceted person with many interests and areas of expertise, you may have dozens of things you could and would love to write about. In terms of marketing your business, focus on areas that appeal to your target audience(s).

What to Write About

We'll begin with a few exercises to help you define what you want to write about.

EXERCISE 1
Your Target Audience's Issues

Get several sheets of paper, or open a word processing document. Write the name of each coaching niche and each target audience you want to work with on the top of a separate page. (Refer to your work in chapter 1.)

Now, write down the interests, goals, challenges and concerns of each niche and target market. If you're not sure, find magazines or websites that publish news of interest to that group and see what they're writing about. Speak with people who represent your target market and find out their concerns. What can *you* write about to address these issues?

You can also look at work you've done with your clients. What are the issues and concerns you've coached them on? Is there a good example or success story that would be the basis for an article that would be interesting to others facing similar challenges?

EXERCISE 2
Topics and Titles

Using the lists from Exercise 1, brainstorm a list of topics and ideas you could, and would enjoy writing about. Turn that into a list of titles for articles you could write that relate to topics your ideal clients would want to read about.

EXERCISE 3
Media List

Finally, research and compile a list of media (magazines, newspapers, newsletters, websites) that would be ideal for your articles. Think about which of these your target audience would be reading. (See Resources for this chapter for media lists.)

With newspapers, find the specific section that would be right for your articles (e.g., Business, Lifestyles, Career). With magazines, contact the Advertising department to get a sales kit with demographic statistics, or look for that information on their websites.

Don't limit yourself to well-known periodicals. There are literally thousands of publications of all sizes that are looking for material to publish. You might do well to start with some of the smaller publications, as well as local or regional ones, to begin building your portfolio of published articles.

And don't forget the Internet. With more people getting information online, the Web is putting many newspapers out of business. Seek out websites that attract your target audience and see if they accept articles. You can also post your work on dedicated articles websites (see Resources for this chapter).

❧

Practice, Practice, Practice

New writers mistakenly expect to write their first article and get it published instantly. Writing takes practice. You need to develop your style and your writing "process." Start by writing about things that are familiar to you, such as your family or your last vacation. Taking a writing class online or in a local continuing education program can help build your competence and your confidence.

If you're already a great writer, practice writing articles geared toward the specific publications where you want to get published.

Don't feel you need to submit your first attempts. Keep writing different articles, until you feel good about your results. Get feedback from trusted friends and colleagues. Then, keep writing and getting your work in front of your audience(s) as often as you can, in the many ways available to you.

HOW TO WORK WITH ARTICLES

Writing

Generating Marketable Ideas

If you've done the exercises earlier in this chapter, you've already got a list of possible articles you could write. In order for those articles to generate leads for coaching clients, they need to speak to a need your audience has.

EXERCISE
Research Topic Ideas

Do some research on the Internet and in those periodicals you're targeting. Which topics on your list are timely or current for your target audience? What new ones would you add to your list? Are there any concerns that haven't hit the media yet that you might be the first to address?

Keep an "ideas" notebook or folder. Include books or websites where you might research each topic or get more information, people you could interview, interesting quotes, etc.

Preparing to Write

Now, it's time to get to work. Choose one of the topics from your list. Select one that excites you and/or one that's easy. Think about:

♦ How can you write about this in a way that's different from what everyone else is doing?

♦ How can you make your article unique?

♦ How can you include your personal perspective or understanding of this topic?

There are a lot of people writing a lot of articles, often about the same timely subjects. Find a way that you can add something fresh, rather than just rehashing what everyone else is saying. If you have a signature writing style, so much the better!

Researching Your Topic

In writing your article, you're not limited to what you already know; you can do research to gather additional information. Begin by compiling everything you currently know about the topic. Use the Internet, books, magazines, newspapers and interviews to flesh out the information you need to write your article.

The Internet is an abundant and convenient way to do research — you can access a wealth of information without leaving your desk — but be wary of the credibility of your sources and check your facts.

Also, while it's okay to take a small quote from your resources, be careful of lifting large sections of text verbatim — that's called plagiarism, and it's a punishable offense. Anything you see in print or on the Internet is copyrighted and the property of the author. Be sure to get permission if you want to use more than a snippet. (If you have any doubt, do a search on "Fair Use" at the U.S. Copyright Office [www.copyright.gov] or contact a publishing or intellectual property lawyer.)

Starting to Write

Choose one of the periodicals in which you'd like to have an article published. Find an article whose style you like — preferably one that's similar to the material you want to write. Read it to get a feel for the style, content, structure, length and format. Estimate the word count. (If you can find the article on the Web, copy the text, paste it into a Word document and use the Word Count tool.)

Most people don't write an article from start to finish in one sitting. It's generally a process. To begin developing your own style of working, try the following:

◆ Begin by outlining or jotting down the key points you want to cover in the article. When ideas come to you, write them out, as scantily or elaborately as you want. Don't worry about form or how well it's written yet.

◆ Now, go back and start fleshing it out. The process that works for me is to write out as much as I can, then put it away and come back to it later or in the next day or so. Each time, I look at it with a fresh eye, add more, and the article begins to take shape.

◆ In terms of structure, a typical structure is to tell your audience what you're going to tell them, then tell them, and conclude with a summary or by drawing a conclusion.

◆ Keep rewriting until the article feels "smooth" to you. Be sure to check for grammar and spelling errors. If you're new at this, or tend to "write rough," get a freelance editor to proofread it and smooth out the rough edges for you.

If you feel you need structure and guidance, consider enrolling in a writing class in a local college or an online writing program such as Gotham Writers' Workshops (see Resources). You can also create an ongoing relationship with an editor, writing coach or virtual assistant with editorial skills to help you with your articles.

To take this seriously, put yourself on a schedule and write on a regular basis. See chapter 10 for more about the writing process.

EXERCISE
Writing Targeted Articles

Using your media list, choose one magazine or newspaper that you would like to target. Get a copy of the periodical and find an article similar to the one you would like to write. Also, go to their website and locate their writers' guidelines or contact the editorial office.

From your list of article titles, select one that would be appropriate for your targeted medium. Write your article, using the process above and the sample article as your model.

Don't stop here. Continue writing and polishing additional articles for various publications.

❧

Your Writing Style

Many people who could enjoy writing articles shy away because they don't feel they're good enough writers. If you're writing fiction or creative non-fiction, certainly your writing style matters. With a non-fiction, self-help piece, it's about conveying the information clearly, not wowing them with your prose.

If you have serious concerns about your writing ability or just don't like to write, you might find a compatible ghost writer or editor who can take your raw ideas and put them into polished form.

Getting Published

Know Your Publication

If you've begun writing, chances are you've already targeted one or more magazines or newspapers to which you'd like to submit your articles.

Learn as much as you can about the publication. Buy several issues and peruse them. With some, you can purchase back issues or find them archived on their website or in the public library.

As you're reviewing the publication, get familiar with the format, writing style, content, etc. Look for:

- The types of articles they publish

- Regular features they include, where you might write a short piece or offer a quote on your area of expertise

- Whether this column or feature is written by a staffer or a freelancer (hint: see if you can find the author's name on the masthead)

- Their demographics — who reads this periodical, including gender, ages, typical occupations, income ranges, geographic location, etc. (This information should be available in their advertising sales kit or writers' guidelines.)

- How often they publish — daily, weekly, monthly, quarterly

- How far in advance you need to submit an article or pitch

- Their editorial calendar — what is the focus of each upcoming issue. This information is generally available a year in advance. On the publication's website, go to the bottom and look for a link such as "Editorial" or "Media Kit."

- How editors prefer to be contacted (phone, e-mail, both)

In addition, you'll want to get the writers' guidelines. If you can't find them on the publication's website, call the editorial office. You can find contact information on the masthead page or on their website. There are also writers' websites with links to guidelines for numerous publications (see Resources). Some of the links may be out-of-date, but it will get you started in your search and give you additional ideas for different periodicals you can approach.

Build a database of publications that relate to your audience and niche. Include the information listed above and any other relevant information that you want to make note of. You can also use your database to keep track of any submissions you make and articles that get published.

EXERCISE
Research Publications

Using the information above, research publications to which you might submit articles that are of interest to your target audience. Compile your notes into a database that you can use to keep track of your submissions and publications.

Pitching

When you're ready to get published, you'll be "pitching" ideas to editors.

When you're approaching editors, remember WIIFM — What's In It For Me. Editors want what *they* want, not necessarily what *you* want to write. Help them do their job. Will your article appeal to their readers? Does it respond to a concern that they have? Is it timely? If you can provide them with good content that fits their needs, they'll come back to you for more.

As a new writer, you'll be building relationships with editors. In the beginning, you'll need to establish your credibility. What expertise or credentials do you have that qualify you to write this article? These can be from formal training or life experience. Until the editor knows you, include a brief bio with your pitch that supports your case.

Unless you have a national "platform" (see chapter 10), a good way to start is with smaller and local publications. This will allow you to start accumulating published writing samples, known as "clips." You can also start with smaller bits, such as contributing an item to a recurring section that features short, newsy items of interest to the reader.

Here are some tips to get you started pitching:

◆ In preparing your pitch, start with an interest-grabbing paragraph: an anecdote, an amazing statistic, a quote establishing that your topic is hot. Demonstrate that you're the perfect person to write this article by establishing your expertise. Close with a summary of how you will approach the article and what exactly you will write about.

◆ Be succinct. Editors are busy people. If you can make your point and keep it short and sweet, so much the better. If they see a long, drawn-out pitch (especially if the first paragraph doesn't grab them) and they don't recognize your name, they may just hit the Delete key.

◆ Make the Subject line of your e-mail clear and compelling. Editors get a lot of e-mail. You need to grab their attention right away and make sure they don't mistake your pitch for yet another piece of SPAM.

◆ Send your pitch to a specific person on the editorial staff. A pitch that is directed to the editorial department, without a specific name, will probably get lost. If possible, find the editor responsible for the area in which you want to be published.

You may want to pitch the editor-in-chief, but keep in mind that that person probably gets the most pitches. Other editorial staff may be able to offer you opportunities as well. If you choose the wrong person, they can point you in the right direction.

It's best to submit a particular idea to one publication at a time. If you don't get a response in a reasonable amount of time, then try another.

◆ E-mail your pitch to the editor you've targeted. Use your business e-mail account, present the pitch as though you were writing a business letter, and use a professional "signature" on your e-mail. Send your pitch and follow up with a phone call to let the editor know it's coming.

♦ Use your database to keep track of where you pitched stories. Include:
  – Publication name
  – Editor's name
  – Date sent
  – Response
  – Any specific feedback you get
  – Any other important notes

Take the time to establish relationships with editors. People like to work with people they know and feel comfortable with. Use any feedback you get to improve your work and better tailor it for their needs. They may not accept your first pitch, but if you're on target with your material and professionally persistent, eventually you'll break through with the publications that are right for you.

EXERCISE
Pitching an Article

Using your research from the previous exercise, target a magazine or newspaper section and craft a pitch for an article that would be appropriate for that publication.

If you want to be daring, go ahead and submit the pitch!

Letting Go

It's important to understand that when you submit your article, it will most likely be changed by the editorial staff. You'll need to do your best, and then get your ego out of the way. No matter how great a writer you are, someone else will always feel they have a better way to present your work. If you're a new writer and don't have the clout, you may need to defer to the editor's changes if you want to be published. You can always ask if it's possible to review the changes before publication.

Publishing on the Internet

Another way to get your articles out there is to submit them to "article directories" on the Internet. Generally, this allows people to reprint your article for free, provided they keep the article and your contact information intact. People also read articles on these sites about various subjects that interest them. By including your Web address, you can lead people back to your website. Having articles placed on various sites also enhances your name recognition.

The Web addresses for some of these directories are included on the Resources list at the end of this chapter. For a more comprehensive list, do a Web search on "article directories." Some listings are free; others charge a fee. You can decide whether it's worth paying.

You can also seek out other websites that work with the same target audience that might want to publish your articles. These should be complementary to what you do, not competitors. It's considered courteous to offer a reciprocal link.

As with printed articles, keep track of the websites where your articles are published. In most cases, it's advantageous to create links from your own website to your articles around the Web. Remember —links both in and out of your website make it more appealing to search engines.

You can also publish your articles on your own website as "added value," to bring people back regularly to read your latest insights.

Does Money Matter?

Some publishing opportunities will be paid, while other will not, or they will offer minimal compensation. While a little extra income never hurts, remember that you're using this opportunity to market your coaching business, so you're receiving "payment" in exposure to potential clients.

As your platform and name recognition grow, you may start targeting high-profile publications. With these, getting paid is a must. At this point, you've built a level of visibility, and charging for your material supports your credibility as a professional.

RESOURCES

The following resources are offered as suggestions, and NOT recommendations. Internet businesses in particular are notorious for changing. If you are considering using any of these vendors, check them out carefully and make an informed decision.

Books

Complete Idiot's Guide to Publishing Magazine Articles, by Sheree Bykofsky and Jennifer Basye Sander

How to Write Articles for Newspapers and Magazines, by Dawn B. Sova

Starting Your Career as a Freelance Writer, by Moira Anderson Allen

Write to Publish: Writing feature articles for magazines, newspapers, and corporate and community publications, by Vin Maskell and Gina Perry

Writer's Digest Handbook of Magazine Article Writing, edited by Michelle Ruberg and Ben Yagoda

Writing Feature Stories: How to Research and Write Newspaper and Magazine Articles, by Matthew Ricketson

Media Lists

Books

Business Organizations, Agencies and Publications Directory
Gale Directory of Publications and Broadcast Media
The International Directory of Little Magazines and Small Presses, by
Len Fulton
Writer's Market (annual)

Websites

Burrells Luce Media Contacts:
www.burrellsluce.com/Media_Contacts/
Easy Media List: www.easymedialist.com
Media Contacts Pro: www.mediacontactspro.com
Media Lists Online: medialistsonline.com

Writing Classes

Gotham Writers' Workshop: www.writingclasses.com
Writers Online Workshops: www.writersonlineworkshops.com
Your local community college or continuing education program

Writers' Guidelines

Freelance Writing: www.freelancewriting.com/guidelines/pages/
Writers Write: www.writerswrite.com/writersguidelines/

Internet Article Sites

Buzzle: www.buzzle.com
Easy Articles: www.easyarticles.com
Ezine @rticles: www.ezinearticles.com
Free Articles Zone: www.free-articles-zone.com
Go Articles: www.goarticles.com
iSnare Articles: www.isnare.com
Self Growth: www.selfgrowth.com/articles.html

There are dozens of sites where you can upload your articles. For additional sites, do a Web search on "submit articles."

Additional Resources

Media Bistro: www.mediabistro.com
Writers Digest: www.writersdigest.com

 **Ten**

Books and E-Books

As the former owner of a small press, and a current writer and self-publisher, this is an area that's close to my heart, and one that I know intimately. When I started publishing in 1990, book publishing seemed like a monumental task. With all the advances in technology in almost two decades, publishing has become accessible to everyone.

Over the years, I've also seen an increase in the number of people who want to, and do, publish a book. My feeling is that in this information age, many of us have knowledge and experience that we want to share, and books are a great way to do that, whether we self-publish or seek out a publisher.

BENEFITS

◆ **Get your message out**

Books are a great way to expose potential clients to your coaching philosophy and programs. Many coach-authors use books to offer starter self-coaching programs that can also encourage readers to take the next step and continue with the support of the coach.

◆ **Gain credibility**

Books are very effective in creating or supporting your "brand." For most people, seeing something in print gives it (and you) credibility. Plus, it's exciting to work with the person who "wrote the book"!

◆ **An entry-level product to get potential clients "in the loop"**

Some people are reluctant to make the large investment that coaching can be without getting to know you first. Once someone has read your book, they'll feel more comfortable moving to the next level and working with you personally.

You can have several different levels of products besides coaching, such as e-booklets, audio programs and book-and-CD self-help programs (as well as workshops — see chapter 12). As "information products," these can be priced higher than trade books and can provide a nice additional income stream.

◆ **A stream of passive income**

There's just so much time in a day to make money. Once a book is written and published, all you need to do is collect your royalties and perhaps fill orders, which can be automated or outsourced.

◆ **An entrée into public speaking**

More and more, having a published book can encourage sponsors to book you for speaking engagements. Once there, you can sell your books "back-of-room." Even with unpaid speaking engagements, you can end up making good money from product sales.

GETTING STARTED

What Should I Write About?

As always, you want to choose a topic that reflects your brand and appeals to your target audience. There may be many things you want, and are able, to write about. In terms of using books as marketing tools, ask:

- What will bring people into my practice?
- Around what types of issues do I want to coach?
- What will people seek me out for?

You can use your book to:

- Demonstrate your expertise
- Solve a problem or fill a need for your target audience
- Create appeal and need for your services

You may fear that by writing a comprehensive book, you're "giving away the store." But people don't always follow through on their own. There are benefits from working with you personally that they can't get from working alone with the book. You're adding your experience, expertise and a perspective that's customized just for them.

In selecting your subject, you may look out in the marketplace and find that every topic you're considering has already been done. That's okay. People who are interested in a particular topic — or in self-help in general — tend to read every book they can get their hands on.

The key is to find a unique approach. Check out the "competition" and see what they've already written. What can you add to the topic? How can you present it differently? Dan Poynter, a self-publishing "guru," was a parachuting aficionado. He wanted to publish a book about it, but it seemed that every aspect of parachuting had already been covered. But nobody had published a comprehensive book that included *all* the information in one volume. And thus, Para Publishing was born.

Your book can also be one aspect of a bigger trademarked program, such as Laura Berman Fortgang's "Now What?®" program or Cheryl Richardson's "Life Makeover Groups™." Your program might include books, audios, workshops and one-on-one coaching. This is a great way to make a name for yourself and offer an array of products and services with a range of price points.

EXERCISE
Book Topics

Make a list of five to ten possible topics for your book. Include any ideas you have about how you might approach each topic in a unique way.

❦

HOW TO WORK WITH BOOKS

The Writing Process

If you've never written before, you'll want to develop a system that will help you stay focused and follow through. The structure I like to use is borrowed from a book called *A Kick in the Seat of the Pants*, by Roger von Oech. The author breaks the creative process down into four phases: Explorer, Artist, Judge and Warrior. Here's how I correlate it to the writing/publishing process:

◆ Explorer: where you research your topic and shape it for your target audience

◆ Artist: the writing phase

◆ Judge: the editing phase

◆ Warrior: where you publish and promote your book

Where I find this structure particularly helpful is as a reminder to stay in the appropriate role. What trips up many writers is bringing in the Judge or the Warrior when they're in the Artist phase — either the Judge is criticizing what they're creating or the Warrior is worrying about whether it will sell.

When you're in the Explorer phase, researching the content and how you will present it, it's fine to take into account what you would like your final product to look like and how you might publish and promote it. But once you're into the Artist phase, you want to give yourself the freedom to create, without the Judge looking over your shoulder or the Warrior worrying about how you're going to get this published. You'll handle those phases later.

Let's look at the four phases in depth.

The Explorer: Doing Research

In the Explorer phase, you'll do several things:

◆ **Research your topic**

If this is something you're choosing to write about, I assume you already have some knowledge and experience with this topic. Use research to flesh out your knowledge and expertise, perhaps getting additional information and other perspectives.

◆ **Research the "competition"**

It's important to be aware of what else is already out there on your topic. You don't want to spend your time duplicating something that's already been done. Explore what others have already done with your topic, to help you find a unique approach.

To research the competition, go to your subject section at the local bookstore and/or library (e.g., Business, Parenting, Self-Help), explore the Books in Print Subject guide (available at libraries and some bookstores), do some keyword searches at online booksellers and look in your personal library. Explore *Publishers Weekly*, either the magazine or online, to see what's current and forthcoming. You may want to purchase some of the significant books you find to add to your personal library of books on your topic.

◆ **Keep marketing in mind**

Before you write your book, think about what the key selling points are. Who is your audience? How can you shape the book to speak to and appeal to them? A book written for academics will be very different from a book written for an audience whose favorite reading is romance novels or for self-help junkies.

◆ **Find your "hook"**

As you're planning your book, keep in mind what your audience is looking for. Are you filling a need or solving a problem they have? Giving them something they desire? Find some relevant keywords, and put them in the title or subtitle of the book.

When my first publishing company was active, we published a wonderful parenting book by Julie Ross. In coming up with a title, I did a brainstorming session with Julie and her husband, Steve. We looked at what we wanted readers to get from the title: We wanted to communicate that the book was practical and that the techniques in the book were forward-thinking and based on current wisdom. What we came up with was, *Practical Parenting for the 21st Century*. The book was published in 1993, and it's still selling today!

EXERCISE 1
Back Cover Copy

A great way to get clarity on the focus of your book is to write the back cover copy. This is a succinct description, often with bullet points, of the content — and benefits — of the book. Pull some books off your shelf that are similar to the type of book you want to write. Turn to the back of the book (or the dustcover flap of a hardcover book). Using these examples, write back cover copy for your book.

EXERCISE 2
Working Title

You may, at this point, also want to come up with a working title for your book. Think of relevant keywords that describe your content and your hook, and brainstorm titles and subtitles.

EXERCISE 3
Format of Your Book

This is also a good time to start thinking about how you want to package your book. Will it be hardcover? Softcover? How big? Will you package it with audio CDs? Will it be printed or an e-book? Continue reading this chapter for ideas.

❧

The Artist: The Creative Writing Process

When your research is complete, you'll move into the Artist phase. Begin by setting up your writing space. Have a comfortable desk, chair and lighting; get your equipment in good working order; line up your reference books; and stock up on supplies.

Create a schedule. Find time when you can work without any distractions. Make your writing a priority, and don't be sidetracked by invitations to go out and play; set aside other time for that. Be aware that writing may take more time than you think, so be realistic about setting goals for completing your work.

EXERCISE
Your Writing Schedule

The best way to get your book done is to work on it regularly. How much time do you want to spend each week working on your book? When is the best time to schedule those hours? Take out your planner and block off that time in your calendar. Take this commitment seriously, and treat it with respect.

❧

A great way to start writing is by creating an outline or structure for your book. Self-help and how-to books often begin by presenting a problem or issue, and then teaching their audience how to solve it. Come up with a structure that leads the reader through in a logical way. If you've created a class or workshop on this topic, you can use it as the basis for your book.

EXERCISE
Creating Your Structure

Write an outline or table of contents for your book. Think about how you would logically present your material so that it has a flow.

Next, think about whether your text needs to be supported by photos, illustrations, examples, exercises, graphs or charts. You don't necessarily need to have these in advance; you can create them once you've mapped out your text. You may also want to include "front matter" (foreword, preface, introduction) and "back matter" (appendixes, resources, reading list or bibliography, author bio, a sales page to promote your coaching and other products, index, etc.).

EXERCISE
Additional Materials

Make a list of additional sections and supporting materials you might want to include in your book. Jot down any ideas you currently have for what you may want to include in those sections.

For your initial draft, just get your thoughts down on paper. Some people write very cleanly from the start, while others will begin with a very rough draft and smooth it out in later versions. Don't expect it to be perfect the first time. Writing is, as they say, in the rewrites.

The key to being in the Artist phase is to give yourself the freedom to let your words pour out, without judging or criticizing them or worrying about what anyone else will think. Once you've got something down on paper, you can move into the Judge phase and use your discernment to fine-tune what you've written.

The Judge: Editing Your Work

"You write with your heart, but you rewrite with your head."
~ from *Finding Forrester*, screenplay by Mike Rich

Once the Artist has done some writing, it's time to bring the Judge into play, bringing a critical eye to your work. I like to make the distinction between "critiquing" — discerning what does and doesn't work and making adjustments — and "criticizing" — shredding your work (and yourself) to pieces. There's no value in just tearing yourself apart. It's about presenting your work in its best light. If this step is difficult for you, you may want to hire an editor or work with a capable, trusted friend.

You may alternate between this phase and the Artist phase, doing some writing, then some editing, going back into the writing phase, then editing again.

It's fine to edit on computer, but at some point, it's important to look at a printout. There are things, such as periods and commas, that are easier to discern from hard copy, rather than on screen.

Once your manuscript feels relatively complete — be careful: you can go on puttering with it forever! — it's important to get another eye (or a few) on your work. No matter how good a writer you are, there are things you'll miss. Whether you plan to submit to an agent or publisher or to self-publish, hire a professional editor to go through your manuscript and give you feedback.

Note that with non-fiction books, if you plan to seek out a publisher, you'll most likely be writing and submitting a proposal *before* you write most of the book. Keep reading this chapter for more on book proposals.

The Warrior: Publishing and Promoting Your Book

In this stage, you'll either be pursuing a publisher or self-publishing. Whichever route you take, you'll also be involved in marketing and promoting your book.

The traditional route to getting published means seeking out an agent or submitting directly to publishers. If you take the self-publishing route, you'll publish through your own company under your own "imprint" or work with an Internet publisher to package your book.

Getting Published vs. Self-Publishing

With self-publishing now an affordable and credible option, you'll need to make a choice as to which route to take. Here are a few aspects to consider:

Getting Published

◆ **Timing**

Traditional publishing takes time. You'll need to write a proposal, query agents or publishers, send the proposal with two to three sample chapters, get a contract and finish writing the book. This can take two to three years. If you want to get your book out faster, consider self-publishing.

◆ **Broad market**

In order to make it worth their investment, large publishing houses need to sell large quantities of books. In order to do that, your topic must have a broad appeal.

◆ **Proposal**

A book proposal is, in itself, a writing project. Your proposal needs to be sharp and professional. In order to have your best chance of getting published, you'll need to budget time to write a great proposal.

◆ **Meeting deadlines**

Once you sign a contract for your book, you'll have to produce it by the allotted deadline. You'll need to be disciplined and able to work under pressure. You may even need to take a sabbatical from your other work and focus on your book for several weeks or months.

◆ **Platform**

Nowadays, most large publishers want authors who already have a "platform." This means that you have established visibility in the marketplace—a website, speaking engagements, other writing credentials, a following. If you're creating a coaching program or brand, you'll want to have these things anyway.

Self-Publishing

◆ **Creative and business control**

One of the primary reasons to self-publish is to retain control. As your own publisher, you have final say on both creative and business decisions. You don't have to fight with your editor over creative choices. You can get your book out as fast as it's ready, and you can keep it in print as long as you want, even if it's only selling ten copies a year. You can market on your own schedule.

◆ **Niche market**

As a small publisher, you can target a particular niche, however small it may be. Without the obligation to reach a broad market, you can gear your book toward the particular audience you want to invite into your coaching practice.

◆ **Quality standard**

Even if you're self-publishing, you want to produce a quality product. It's worth spending a little extra money to hire an editor (a poorly-constructed book filled with typos doesn't do much for your professional image) and get an attractive book cover design.

◆ **Investment / additional business responsibilities**

As a self-publisher, you'll be footing the bill for the production of your book. Along with production costs, it may involve adding additional functions to your existing business. The good news is, there are lots of affordable support options out there.

◆ **Resources and support**

The small press movement has been around for quite awhile now, so there are lots of resources and support. The Independent Book Publishers Association is the prime organization for small and self-publishers, offering resources, support and marketing opportunities (see Resources for this chapter).

◆ **Technology and Internet publishers**

The advent of digital printing and Internet publishers has made publishing easy and affordable. An Internet publisher can do the production work for you — and assist with the marketing — for a reaonable cost.

Now, let's look at what's involved in taking either of these routes.

Getting Published

◆ **Agent vs. publisher**

If you're planning to approach big publishers with wide distribution channels, you'll need an agent. Many publishers have cut back on their editorial staff. They don't have time to screen unsolicited manuscripts, so they count on ongoing relationships with trusted agents, who screen submissions for them.

If you're planning to submit to a smaller publisher, you may be able to submit directly to an editor at the company. A smaller company may not have as much clout, but you often get more attention and support, and they may keep your book in print longer.

Pick up a current copy of the *Writers Market* (or subscribe to their online service), or do some research on the Web, and check out the submission policies of the publishers or agents you're considering.

You might also consider going to a publishing conference. Book Expo America, the major conference in the United States, takes place annually around Memorial Day. Check their website (www.bookexpoamerica.com) for current information.

There are also many smaller writers' conferences. Here in New York, we have the International Women's Writing Guild (www.iwwg.org). Their weekend conferences in April and October afford writers the opportunity to meet with agents who support the organization and are open to receiving new submissions. Do some Web searches to see what's available in other areas (see Resources). What fun it would be to plan a vacation in Maui and attend the writers' conference there (www.mauiwriters.com)!

◆ **Do your research**

You're more likely to impress an agent and be effective in connecting with the right one if you do your research. Agents specialize in different types of books, or "genres." Do your homework and find agents in your category. Go to bookstores and find the section where your book would be shelved. Pull some out and turn to the Acknowledgments page — many authors thank their agent and editor. You can also go to agents' websites and look at the list of book contracts they've brokered (see Resources).

◆ **Target your efforts**

Be strategic about who you contact. An agent or publisher who doesn't work in your genre isn't going to take time to look at your proposal. Don't waste your time or theirs.

◆ **Submit to a specific person**

It's always best to direct your submission to a specific person. Whether you're submitting to an agent or a publisher, get a name. For publishing companies, consult the *Writers Market* or the *Literary Marketplace* to get the name of the editor best suited for your project. For agents, consult a current agents' guide in print or on the Web (see Resources).

◆ **Proposals vs. queries**

In seeking a publisher or agent, you'll be submitting a proposal. Some prefer that you begin with a "query," which is a condensed version, no longer than three pages or an equivalent e-mail. Check their submission guidelines to see which they prefer, or use your own judgment about how you can best present your book. (See the Resources and search online bookstores for books on proposal writing.)

With nonfiction books, you'll generally write the proposal *before* the book is finished. Editors want to have a hand in shaping your book. You don't want to finish writing your book, only to have the editor who signed you ask for a major change. The proposal also helps you think out the different aspects of your book in greater detail.

Components of a Book Proposal

A book proposal is a writing project in itself. This is your "sales document." You want to make a good first impression and fill it with information that packs a wallop and shows your book in its best light.

While you do have some creative leeway with proposals, there are several standard components.

◆ **Cover letter**

Since most proposals are now submitted electronically, your "cover letter" is the body of the e-mail. Even so, structure it like a business letter, addressing it to the specific person you're approaching and including a full signature and contact information. Believe it or not, when I was publishing, I received e-mail queries that weren't signed.

For the Subject line, write: "Requested Proposal" and the name of your book.

Your cover letter should have a strong opening — you need to catch their attention in the first sentence or paragraph. You can do this by using a provocative line, a story or anecdote, or a startling statistic. One of my favorites is from astronaut Pete Conrad: "I did not sleep very well the night before I went to the moon."

Keep your cover letter brief. Its purpose is simply to entice the reader to continue on and read your proposal, which includes the bulk of the important information.

The rest of your proposal will be sent, upon request, as an attached Microsoft Word document.

◆ **Title page**

Include the book title, your name and contact information.

◆ **Overview or summary**

In this first section of the proposal, you'll expound on the theme of your book, the important elements and how the book is organized. For example, your book may be built around client success stories or interviews, with chapters organized by the area of success, such as career, family, finances, self-care, etc.

In this section, you also need to address any obvious obstacles or issues. For example, if your book requires interviews with former presidents of the United States, you need to demonstrate that you have access to them.

◆ **Author information**

Here, you present your credentials — what qualifies you to write this book. While advanced degrees are always impressive, your credibility may also come from professional or life experience in the area related to your topic. You just need to be able to convey a level of expertise in what you're writing about.

More and more, "ordinary" people who are not professionals in the field are writing about their experiences and what they've learned from them, such as parenting books or books about dealing with a particular medical or life challenge. Non-professionals who have gone through a certain life experience can offer a perspective that professionals may lack, despite their education and training. In these instances, it doesn't hurt to get an endorsement or a foreword from a professional in a related field to support your case.

◆ Marketing

Your potential publisher will want to know who you expect to buy this book — this will probably be the same audience you're targeting for your coaching practice. Your future publisher will also want to know what you're providing for this group that's not already out in the marketplace. This may be something new, such as a program you've created, or useful information presented in a unique way. It's helpful to provide market research or statistics that support the need for this material.

◆ Competition

Your publisher will also want to know what's already out there on your topic, and how your book compares. While you may feel that this information should be readily available, it's a research job that takes time and effort. Don't expect your publisher (or agent) to do that for you or assume that they already know — you know your field better than they do. Also, by doing your own homework, you can more skillfully make a case that your book is different and somehow better than the existing competition.

◆ Promotion

In this section, you'll let your publisher know how you plan to promote your book. While larger publishers do have marketing departments, you'll be expected to support and enhance their efforts. You'll do this by establishing your "platform"—how you will become visible to buyers via your website(s), speaking engagements, other books, articles you have written or will write and so on.

◆ **Chapter outline or "annotated table of contents"**

This is the meat of the proposal, where you convince the editor that your book is worth publishing. In this section, you'll outline the entire book, chapter by chapter. Include some detail, although it will not be written out fully, as your sample chapters will be.

◆ **Sample chapters**

To give a sample of your writing (particularly if this is your first book), you'll include one to three chapters of your book, depending on the length of the chapters. I would recommend consecutive chapters, probably from the beginning, to give the reader a sense of the flow. Take time to make sure that these chapters are well-written and polished. No matter how great your subject matter, if your writing is sloppy and not well-thought-out, you won't make a sale. Editors no longer have time to nurture a promising author, unless they expect a blockbuster.

If you have concerns about your writing ability, you might want to take on a writing partner or hire a ghostwriter or editor to help you shape your material.

◆ **Anything else you need to include**

Here, you may include anything that supports your manuscript, such as a few sample photos or illustrations (never send originals!) or a copy of an article that you've had published on this topic. Your proposal may already be quite thick, so you don't want to include anything that doesn't directly support your case.

You may also want to include a note about the "delivery"—how long it will take, once the contract is signed, for you to deliver a finished manuscript. Remember—non-fiction book proposals are generally written *before* the book is completed, to allow your editor to have input on the final product.

In the rare case that your proposal is submitted by "snail mail," it is expected that you will include a stamped, self-addressed envelope for the editor or agent to use to respond to your submission.

There are several books and online resources that offer detailed instructions on writing proposals. My favorite is Jeff Herman's book, *Write the Perfect Book Proposal.* I particularly like this book because it includes several actual samples that show you what to do, rather than just telling you.

Why Self-Publish?

At one time, self-publishing carried a stigma. Many of the books published by "vanity presses" were badly written, unedited and filled with typos. Digital technology has made self-publishing affordable for most individuals, and Internet publishers provide the editing and design services that were previously overlooked, along with support in marketing.

With many good authors jumping on the self-publishing bandwagon — and effectively marketing their books via the Internet — self-publishing has gained a new credibility. If you prefer to "cut to the chase" and get your book in print yourself, rather than running the gauntlet of finding a publisher, self-publishing is an excellent option. Another plus: With cutbacks in editorial staff, publishers often look to successful self-published books for new products.

Self-publishing is actually a proud tradition. Virginia and Leonard Woolf founded Hogarth Press in 1917, printing their books from a printing press on their kitchen table for almost 30 years. Previously, Beatrix Potter unleashed Peter Rabbit on the world herself, prompting publisher Frederick Warne to become her publisher (and husband!). Mark Twain, annoyed with his publisher, published *Huckleberry Finn* himself, releasing it as a serial to 40,000 subscribers.

More-contemporary authors, among the many who found success by initially self-publishing, include Ken Blanchard (*The One-Minute Manager*), James Redfield (*The Celestine Prophecy*), Richard Nelson Bolles (*What Color Is Your Parachute?*), Tom Peters (*In Search of Excellence*) and Irma Rombauer (*The Joy of Cooking*).

Your Own Imprint vs. Using an Internet Publisher

When I began publishing in 1990, starting your own company, or "imprint," was the only option for a self-publisher. If you choose this route and already have a coaching business, you could have a publishing "division." Having your own imprint gives you access to some services reserved only for publishers, but it does require an investment of time and money.

Many coaches are choosing to work with an Internet publisher. For a pretty reasonable price, these companies provide document layout, basic cover design, book production and some sales and marketing. You can upgrade your cover and purchase additional services, such as editing and expanded marketing, for additional fees, or you can find your own vendors.

If you're busy, or only publishing a handful of titles, working with an Internet publisher may be expedient for you. Writing a book takes a concerted effort, and once the manuscript is done, you may prefer to hand over the rest of the job to someone else. If you want to start your own company, there are numerous books on the market about self-publishing and business start-up.

Choosing An Internet Publisher

Selecting an Internet publisher is like comparing apples and oranges. Each publisher has its own set of services and ways of packaging those services.

Following are some questions to ask Internet publishers in order to gather the information that will help you make the best choice. (A glossary of common publishing terms follows.)

- What is the setup cost? What's included in the basic package? Are there different levels of packages? How do they compare? What do I really need?

- What additional services are offered, such as editing, indexing and enhanced cover design?

- What trim sizes are available? (Typical sizes are 6" x 9", 5 ½" x 8 ½" and 8 ¼" x 11".) What is the additional cost for alternative sizes?

- If applicable: Do you offer color printing for the book text?

- How do you determine the retail price of the book?

- How many copies are included in the basic package? What will it cost me to purchase additional books? Do you offer a discount for quantity purchases?

- What kinds of distribution do you offer — through your own Web store, online retailers, bookstores, etc.?

- What royalty rate will I receive when my books sell?

- What options do you offer for marketing my book? What's included in the basic package and what's extra?

- What is the turnaround time for publishing my book?

- Will my book also be available as an e-book? Is there an extra charge for this?

    Also:

- Ask to see a copy of their contract (or download it from their website, if available), and read it thoroughly, so you know what you're agreeing to. NEVER give away the copyright of your book to an Internet publisher.

- Check out their customer service. Some companies have aggressive sales departments, but once you sign on the dotted line, it's like pulling teeth to get through to customer service and get support.

◆ Ask for references, or better yet, go to their Web store, get the names of some of the authors, contact them directly (do a search to find their websites) and ask if they'll speak with you about their publishing experience with this company.

◆ Consider any additional expenses you will incur that fall outside the basic package, such as editing, indexing, enhanced cover design, marketing and the purchase of additional books for your own use or resale. Some companies charge a fee for processing returns (see Publishing Terms below).

See appendix B for a form you can use to compare the information you gather from various Internet publishers.

EXERCISE
How Should I Publish?

Now that you know the ins and outs of publishing vs. self-publishing, think about which path would work best for you. You might make a pros-and-cons list for each.

❧

Publishing Terms

Here are some terms that are useful to know, whether you're publishing through your own company or working with an Internet publisher.

◆ **Offset printing** — This is the process typically used for printing books. Pricing is based on the setup cost plus the cost of paper and ink. Since the setup cost is the same, no matter how many copies you print, the more you print, the lower the **cost per book** (the total cost of printing divided by the number of copies). If you publish less than 500 copies (if the company will even do it), the cost per book gets high.

◆ **Print-on-Demand (POD)** — This refers to digital printing. The "setup" generally consists of creating PDF files of the "book block" and the cover. While some POD printers charge higher prices for smaller quantities, in truth, once the book is set up, the process is the same whether they print one book or a thousand. The beauty of POD is that you can print books as you need them, thus reducing the need for warehousing large quantities of books, as well as the risk of ending up with excess inventory that you can't sell.

◆ **Trim size** — This is the size of the book as you view it from the front. Typical trim sizes for trade books are 6" x 9" and 5 ½" x 8 ½".

◆ **Page count** — This is the number of pages in the book, counting each side of the page, as well as any blank and unnumbered pages. The cost of producing the book will be based on the trim size and page count. With POD printing, some printers will charge for blank pages, others will not.

◆ **Binding** — This is the way the pages of the book are held together. The most common bindings are hardcover and trade paperback. You may also see spiral-bound and other types of binding. Bookstores prefer bindings that have the title printed on the spine, as the books are often displayed spine out.

◆ **Spine** — This is the view of the book you generally have when it's on the bookshelf in a library or bookstore. A book with more pages or heavier paper will have a wider spine. With POD printing, most companies will not print titles on the spine if your book is less than 64 pages — digital printing is not as precise as offset printing, so with a narrow spine, they can't guarantee that the title will be centered. This can be a problem if you want to sell to bookstores and libraries.

◆ **Dust jacket** — This is the paper jacket you see on hardcover books. As the author/publisher, you'll need to provide additional copy, and perhaps a picture, for the flyleaf. Hardcover books also have printing or embossing on the binding of the book itself, whether it be on fabric or paper. Look at some hardcover books in your library for examples.

♦ **Text: paper stock and ink** — Most publishing houses have standard papers that they use. For general text, they usually have a 55# [pound] natural, or something similar. Photo books may be printed on glossy, bright white paper. Text ink is usually black, although some printers can do color printing for photography or children's books (which is, of course, more expensive).

♦ **Cover: paper stock, ink and lamination** — Cover stock will often be 10 pt or 12 pt (the weight or thickness), and designated as C1S (meaning that it's coated on one side). With offset printing, more colors means more passes through the press and greater expense. Full color printing is usually done in four passes, although a creative designer can come up with an imaginative design with fewer colors. With digital printing, the number of colors doesn't matter. Covers are usually laminated on the printed side for protection.

♦ **Front matter** — Literally, the "matter" at the front of the book, including such things as: introduction, foreword, preface, table of contents, dedication, acknowledgments, etc.

♦ **Back matter** — The "matter" at the back of the book, such as: appendixes, bibliography, glossary, index, author biography, etc.

♦ **ISBN** — This is the International Standard Book Number, a unique number that identifies a particular book in the inventory system. Each publisher has a unique "prefix," followed by additional numbers that identify that particular book. The ISBN is represented on the book by a bar code. In 2007, the publishing industry moved from a 10-digit to a 13-digit ISBN system. On books published during the transition period, you'll often see both printed on the copyright page and by the bar code on the back cover.

♦ **Library of Congress** — The Library of Congress, along with archiving books, provides information that is useful to libraries that are cataloguing your book:

– **Preassigned Control Number (PCN)** — This is a 10-digit number that you'll find on the copyright page of the book. The number is provided for free upon application (see Resources). Once the book is published, the PCN becomes the **LCCN (Library of Congress Control Number)**.

– **Cataloging-in-Publication data (CIP)** — This is the information that tells the librarian how to categorize your book and where to file it in their library. You'll also find this on the copyright page of many books.

Because of the overwhelming number of books being published, the Library of Congress does not provide CIP data for self-published books. If you plan to sell to libraries, it would be a worthwhile investment to have CIP data prepared by Quality Books or another qualified source (see Resources).

This information is not required, but it can be useful in encouraging libraries to purchase your book.

◆ **Imprint** — This is the name of the publishing entity, which appears on the title and copyright pages, as well as the spine of the book. With a small company, the name of the company is generally also the imprint. A large company will have several imprints. For example, Harper Collins is also the umbrella for William Morrow, Avon, Greenwillow and numerous other imprints.

◆ **Print run** — This is the number of books that are printed in each order. With offset printing, a print run probably wouldn't be smaller than 500. With POD, the print run can be as small as one book. Remember — with offset printing, the larger the print run, the lower the cost per book, but overprinting can leave you with a warehouse of unsold books.

◆ **Returns** — In the publishing industry, a book is not sold until it is in the hands of the consumer. Book retailers and wholesalers reserve the right to return any unsold books to the publisher or distributor, and they often come back in unsaleable condition. While this can wreak havoc with your financials and waste good books, it also encourages bookstores to take a chance on a book that might not sell. Many POD publishers have set up systems to deal with returns, sometimes for an additional charge; some simply sell on a nonreturnable basis.

Selling and Marketing Your Book

Whether you self-publish or get published, you'll be participating in the marketing efforts for your book. If you're self-publishing, you'll also be involved in selling. This is a quick overview of some book marketing concepts. See the Resources section of this chapter for additional resources.

Book Sales

If you're targeting bookstores, your best bet is to connect with a small press distributor. You can find these in the *Literary Marketplace* or on the Independent Book Publishers Association website (www.ibpa-online.org — click on Publishers Resources). You may also be able sell through wholesalers, such as Baker & Taylor (www.btol.com) and Ingram (www.ingrambook.com).

There are many places to sell books besides bookstores. These include:

♦ **Libraries** — Public and school libraries.

♦ **Book clubs** — These may be general interest clubs, like Book-of-the-Month, or focused by special interest, such as One Spirit.

♦ **Catalogs** — Look for catalogs specifically for books, as well as others that are related to your topic, such as a catalog that sells an array of career-related items.

♦ **Stores related to your subject** — This might be a store that specializes in products on leadership or health-related items.

♦ **Price clubs** — These outlets tend to buy in quantity products that are of broad interest.

♦ **Direct to consumer** — You can sell your book directly to the reader from your website, through direct mail or back-of-room at speaking engagements.

◆ **Special markets** — With a little focused effort, you can sell quantities of your book to corporations to use for staff training or as incentive giveaways to customers.

◆ **Foreign sales** — Many foreign publishers seek out popular U.S. books and purchase "translation rights." The greatest outlet for these sales is the Frankfurt Book Fair (www.frankfurt-book-fair.com), held annually in October.

◆ **Subsidiary ("sub") rights** — This category includes electronic, periodical, translation and film/TV rights. For some of these, you'll want an agent to represent you.

◆ **Affiliate programs** — These are a way to get others to sell your books and earn commissions. The affiliate has a link on their website that uses a coded URL that takes the buyer to the book page on your website. When a sale is made, it is recorded by the Web company—the one that provides the coded links—which processes the sale and distributes the commission. See the Resources section for a list of some of these companies.

You can also become an affiliate of Amazon by joining Amazon Associates and earning commissions by promoting other books through your website (see Resources).

EXERCISE
Outlets for Selling My Book

Select the outlets through which you would like to sell your book.
- ❏ Bookstores
- ❏ Libraries
- ❏ Book clubs
- ❏ Catalogs
- ❏ Stores
- ❏ Price clubs
- ❏ Direct to consumer

❑ Special markets
❑ Foreign sales
❑ Subsidiary rights
❑ Affiliate programs
❑ _____

Book Marketing

When marketing books, you need to keep in mind that you're marketing on two fronts: to the trade and to the consumer. You market to the trade to get your book into bookstores and other outlets where people can purchase your book. You market to the consumer to entice them into the store to actually purchase your book. Remember — retailers have the right to return your books if they don't sell, so you need to market to the end user to complete the sale.

Some types of marketing that you might consider include:

◆ **Advertising** — You can place ads in newspapers, magazines, consumer catalogs, distributors' and wholersalers' catalogs, as well as on the Web.

◆ **Reviews** — Submit your book for review to trade publications, such as *Publishers Weekly, Library Journal* or *Booklist*; to websites that feature book reviews; and to the book section of publications or the section relevant to your topic (e.g., business, career, lifestyles). Get their guidelines from the website or editorial office to find out how and what to submit.

◆ **Direct mail** — You can do mass mailings to your own database or purchase a targeted list from a list broker. Plan to do mailings on a regular basis to get significant sales.

◆ **Cooperative efforts** — Join with other publishers to share the cost of ads or mailings. The Independent Book Publishers Association (www.ibpa-online.org) offers cooperative marketing opportunities to members, where you split the expense with other publishers.

- **Press releases** — Use news releases to notify media outlets of your new book. Find a way to make it newsworthy to catch their attention! (See chapter 14 for more on working with media.)

- **Media appearances on TV and radio** — If you're comfortable with public appearances, they're a great way to get the word out about your book. A great resource is the *Radio-TV Interview Report* (www.rtir.com), where you can advertise your book and area of expertise to TV and radio hosts. (See chapter 14 for more on working with media.)

- **Book signings / readings** — Aside from bookstores, you might schedule book signings, along with a lecture or reading, at libraries, adult learning centers and adult education programs at universities.

- **Speaking engagements** — Many organizations are constantly looking for speakers. These may include learning centers, civic groups, professional networking groups, men's and women's groups, religious and spiritual groups, youth groups, spas and health clubs. You can offer something of value while promoting your book and, in most cases, sell your book "back of room" after the lecture. (See chapter 12 for more on speaking.)

- **Workshops related to the topic of your book** — If you like to teach, you can develop workshops around the topic of your book to entice people to purchase the book (and maybe to sign up for coaching!). (See chapter 12 for more on workshops.)

- **Website** — Even if you have a website for your coaching business, you may want to have a separate website where the domain name is the name of your book. If you're working with a publisher (traditional or Internet), they will also include your book on their website.

- **Articles or excerpts published in magazines, newspapers and websites** — You can write articles related to the topic of your book or grant reprint rights of a section or chapter for print publications or the Web. (See chapter 9 for more on working with articles.)

EXERCISE
Ways to Market My Book

Select the ways that you would like to market your book.

❑ Advertising

❑ Reviews

❑ Direct mail

❑ Cooperative efforts

❑ Press releases

❑ Media appearances

❑ Book signings / readings

❑ Speaking engagements

❑ Workshops

❑ Website

❑ Articles or excerpts

❑ _____

❑ _____

E-Books, Booklets and Reports

Another form of publishing is e-books and booklets, generally distributed as PDF documents. While there are mixed opinions about reading entire books from a computer screen, e-publications do have several benefits.

Benefits

◆ **Easy to produce**

E-books can be created easily and inexpensively using word processing or page layout software and then converted to a PDF file. They can be anything from a one-page report to a full-length book. You can use a simple title page or hire someone to create a more artistic cover design, and there is no expense for producing copies (although you can also package them on a CD-ROM for in-person sales).

♦ **Ability to add enhancements**

With a PDF management program such as Adobe Acrobat (the full version, not Adobe Reader), you can protect your e-document so that it can't be modified. You can add bookmarks, so readers can easily find their way to a specific page; create fill-in forms; and add hyperlinks to bring your reader to a particular Internet page to get additional information or find a resource. If you are an Amazon affiliate, you can use your affiliate link for the reader to click through, so that you receive a commission on anything they purchase on that visit.

Readers with the full version of Acrobat can also add notes and highlight or underline text in the document.

♦ **Easy to store and fill orders**

With e-books, there's no inventory to store, and filling orders is as easy as sending an e-mail attachment. If you have a brisk enough business to make it cost-effective, you can use a shopping cart service that fills orders automatically, and you can sit back and collect the income.

From the reader's perspective, e-books don't take up any "real" space, and (if you allow it in the security settings) they can print out all or parts of the document.

♦ **Portability**

With so many people traveling and commuting, e-books can be loaded onto a laptop or dedicated reader (such as Amazon's Kindle) and taken wherever they go. This allows you to have dozens of books on one device. Downloadable books also tend to be cheaper than their printed counterparts.

Uses of E-Books

E-books are excellent for both product sales and as giveaways to promote your practice. They can be used in a variety of ways:

◆ **Full-length books**

E-books can be standalone items or alternative versions of your printed books.

◆ **Booklets and reports**

E-booklets are a great way to "package" articles, reports or short publications, such as tips booklets. As an **informational product**, with information that is valuable to the purchaser, you might charge as much — or more — for a ten-page article as you could for a full-length trade book.

◆ **Giveaways**

The use of giveaways is a great marketing strategy — people always appreciate that you're freely sharing something of value. E-books are an easy way to do this at little or no cost. You might offer a free article or report when people sign up for your newsletter. You can share a quiz, checklist or tool that teaches your potential clients about themselves and draws them to your website to learn more about your coaching services.

Giveaways can be set up on an autoresponder (check with your website or shopping cart host), so that your prospects receive them without requiring any of your time.

◆ **Promotional materials**

While a website is still your best informational tool, you can have your brochure or one-sheet in PDF format, so that you can e-mail it when requested. If prospective clients tend to ask the same questions over and over again, you might create a FAQs PDF that you can send when you respond to inquiries about your coaching services. (See chapter 13 on promotional materials.)

◆ **Client materials**

If you use forms, worksheets, handouts or welcome packets with your clients — especially if your practice is non-local — you can put them together as PDFs and e-mail them to your clients.

E-books also lend themselves very well to workbooks. Clients can print out clean copies of worksheets as needed, or you can set it up so that they can do the worksheets right in the document, using fill-in forms.

EXERCISE
How I Can Use E-Books

Check off the ways you could utilize e-books to enhance your marketing efforts and coaching practice.

❑ Full-length books
❑ Booklets and reports
❑ Giveaways
❑ Promotional materials
❑ FAQs page for prospective clients
❑ Client forms, worksheets, handouts
❑ Welcome packet
❑ Workbooks
❑ _____

RESOURCES

The following resources are offered as suggestions, and NOT recommendations. Internet businesses in particular are notorious for changing. If you are considering using any of these vendors, check them out carefully and make an informed decision.

Books

How to Get Happily Published: A Complete and Candid Guide, by Judith Appelbaum

Write the Perfect Book Proposal: 10 That Sold and Why, by Jeff Herman, Deborah Levine Herman

How to Write a Book Proposal, by Michael Larsen

Making the Perfect Pitch: How to Catch a Literary Agent's Eye, by Katharine Sands

2009 Guide to Literary Agents, by Chuck Sambuchino

How to Get a Literary Agent, by Michael Larsen

Writer's Market (updated annually)

Literary Marketplace (updated annually)

Dan Poynter's Self-Publishing Manual: How to Write, Print, and Sell Your Own Book, by Dan Poynter

The Complete Guide to Self Publishing: Everything You Need to Know to Write, Publish, Promote, and Sell Your Own Book, by Tom and Marilyn Ross

How To Publish and Promote Online, by M. J. Rose and Angela Adair-Hoy

1001 Ways to Market Your Books: For Authors and Publishers, by John Kremer

The Complete Guide to Book Publicity, by Jodee Blanco

Publicize Your Book!: An Insider's Guide to Getting Your Book the Attention It Deserves, by Jacqueline Deval

A Kick in the Seat of the Pants: Using Your Explorer, Artist, Judge, & Warrior To Be More Creative, by Roger von Oech

Trade Publications (also for reviews)

Publishers Weekly: www.publishersweekly.com

Library Journal: www.libraryjournal.com

Booklist: www.ala.org/booklist *and* www.booklistonline.com

Writing and Publishing Conferences and Fairs

Book Expo America: www.bookexpoamerica.com
Frankfurt Book Fair: www.frankfurt-book-fair.com
International Women's Writing Guild: www.iwwg.org
Guide to Writers Conferences and Workshops:
    writing.shawguides.com

Literary Agent Databases

Association of Authors' Representatives:
    www.aar-online.org/mc/page.do
Agent Query: www.agentquery.com
Literary Agents E-mail Addresses:
    www.writers-free-reference.com/agents/index.html
Preditors & Editors: anotherealm.com/prededitors/pubagent.htm
WritersNet: www.writers.net/agents.html

E-Publishers

Authorhouse: www.authorhouse.com
Booklocker: www.booklocker.com
Bookstand Publishing: www.ebookstand.com
Infinity Publishing: www.infinitypublishing.com
iUniverse: www.iUniverse.com
Trafford: www.trafford.com
Universal Publishers: www.universal-publishers.com
Unlimited Publishing: www.unlimitedpublishing.com
Writer's Collective: www.writerscollective.org
Xlibris: www2.xlibris.com
Blurb: www.blurb.com (download software, create your own book)

Publishing with Amazon Advantage

On Demand Publishing (CreateSpace and BookSurge):
advantage.amazon.com/gp/vendor/public/join/

Self-Publishing Resources

Independent Book Publishers Association: www.ibpa-online.org
Small Publishers Association of North America: www.spannet.org
Para Publishing / Dan Poynter: www.parapublishing.com
Book Marketing Update / John Kremer: bookmarket.com
Library of Congress: pcn.loc.gov
Quality Books (Cataloging-in-Publication data):
www.quality-books.com/pcip.htm
Five Rainbows: www.fiverainbows.com
Self-Publishing: www.selfpublishing.com
Get Known Now/Suzanne Falter-Barnes: www.getknownnow.com

Designers and Editors

Guru: www.guru.com
Elance: www.elance.com
Coroflot: www.coroflot.com
Creative Hot List: www.creativehotlist.com

PDF Software

Adobe Acrobat (Mac and PC): www.adobe.com/products/acrobat/
PDF Converter Professional (PC): www.nuance.com/products/
PDFEdit (PC – free): www.pdf995.com/pdfedit.html
PDFpen (Mac): www.smileonmymac.com/PDFpen/

Booklets

Tips Products International / Paulette Ensign:
  www.tipsbooklets.com
E-booklet Directory: www.ebookletdirectory.com

Affiliate Programs and Management

Amazon Associates:
  affiliate-program.amazon.com/gp/ associates/join
1ShoppingCart: www.1shoppingcart.com
Payloadz: www.payloadz.com
3d Cart: www.3dcart.com

 **ELEVEN**

AUDIOS AND VIDEOS

With everyone wired to their electronic gadgets nowadays, audio and video products are a great way to reach your audience.

BENEFITS

◆ **Give clients a "live" experience of you**

The best way to market coaching is to give potential clients a live, direct experience of you. A recording is the next best thing.

◆ **Establish your expertise**

As with books, having a published product in which you speak about a particular topic establishes you as an expert in the mind of the listener.

◆ **Additional income stream**

Along with printed products, audios and videos can be a great addition to your product line and increase your passive income potential.

◆ **Sell at speaking engagements**

Some of your audience would prefer to see and hear you, rather than just read your words on the page. Audios and videos give them the opportunity to take that home with them.

◆ **Entry level products to bring clients into the loop**

Along with books, recorded products are lower-priced items that help potential clients feel secure with who you are, your message and your competence level. This encourages them to take the next step and hire you as a coach.

◆ **Add audio and video clips to your website to make it more dynamic**

Along with having your picture on your website, hearing your voice or seeing a moving image brings clients one step closer to the real you. Many people are also getting great exposure by uploading professional videos, such as an interview about coaching, to YouTube.

GETTING STARTED

Exploring Audios and Videos

It's always helpful to explore what others are doing to get ideas for your own products and see what you like and don't like. Go to the "Products" or "Store" section of coaches' websites, and perhaps purchase a few samples to review.

For high-end products, check out the Hay House website (www.hayhouse.com), which includes products from some well-known coaches, including Cheryl Richardson, Debbie Ford and Michael Neill.

Creating Content

There are several ways you can create material for your audio or video. As with other tools, you want to choose topics that support your brand.

◆ **Write a program**

You can write out a program, and perhaps a full script, just as you would for a live presentation.

◆ **Do an interview**

Interview someone, or have someone interview you, and record it. Prepare the questions, and the general content of the responses, ahead of time, so you have some idea of the flow of the interview. Then, let go and be creative.

◆ **Record a class or teleclass**

If you're doing a live class or a teleclass, record it. Teleclasses are easy — many conference line services (also called "bridge lines") incorporate recording ability, or you can use a recording service like Audio Acrobat. With a live class, you can wire yourself to a digital audio recorder, or use a professional service to capture both your lecture and your audience's participation (be sure to get releases!), whether just the audio or as a video.

HOW TO WORK WITH AUDIOS AND VIDEOS

Preparation

Unless you're an experienced speaker who's brilliantly spontaneous, it's best to prepare and rehearse your material. At the very least, prepare a flow outline and structure for your presentation.

Practice your microphone technique, and practice recording the material, so it sounds clear and natural. Capture your video rehearsal with your camcorder. Play it back, and look for places where you could improve your delivery or content, as well as your personal presentation (clothes, hair, makeup, posture, where you're focusing your eyes, etc.).

See chapter 8 on Podcasts for more on preparing and recording.

Recording – Audios

Home technology has gotten so good that you can record a pretty decent quality audio from home. You need a good microphone, along with a good recorder (preferably digital) or recording software on your computer. (See chapter 8 on Podcasts for more about recording.) You can also record using a conference line with recording capability or a service such as Audio Acrobat. Test out the service or software to get the best quality. (Tip: For better sound, record using a USB microphone, rather than over the phone.)

Once the recording is complete, you'll need to edit it — to cut out any fluffed sections or undesirable "ums" and "ahs," as well as adding a standard opening and closing, perhaps with music. You can use software such as Audacity or GarageBand to do this, or find a professional audio engineer.

If you have the budget and want to make a high-end product, you can record in a professional studio and have the recording professionally edited. Search online or consult your local Yellow Pages for studios in your area.

Recording – Videos

Videos are (obviously) harder to do yourself. If you have a good digital camcorder and microphone, an appropriate space and a trusted friend, you can come up with a decent product. For something slicker, you'll want to hire someone to record your lecture in a studio, or have them video your class or speaking engagement on site.

Computer cams are fine for short video clips to put on your website, but not for a high quality product. In either case, make sure you have an appropriate background — DO NOT record with your messy office or your kids' artwork in the background.

You can edit your video on your computer, using software such as Final Cut Pro, or have it done professionally.

Packaging

There are three options for getting your audio or video to your customer.

◆ **As a streaming audio or video from your website**

This may be a free clip or a paid product. For the latter, purchasers will receive a link and a password to access the audio or video. Work with your Web designer to set this up.

◆ **Low volume, low budget, do-it-yourself**

If you're only selling small quantities of your product, you can burn individual CDs or DVDs from your computer. To package them, purchase jewel boxes or cases, design simple labels and case inserts and print them on a color printer.

◆ **High volume, high quality, mass produced**

For high volume commercial production, there are companies that design, duplicate and package CDs and DVDs (see the Resources for some suggestions). You can also purchase high-volume duplication equipment, but if you choose this route, remember to factor in your time or the cost of hiring someone to do the work.

Exercise
Creating an Audio or Video

Using the information in this chapter, plan, record and package an audio or video clip or product.

❦

RESOURCES

The following resources are offered as suggestions, and NOT recommendations. Internet businesses in particular are notorious for changing. If you are considering using any of these vendors, check them out carefully and make an informed decision.

AUDIO

Recording Services and Conference Lines

Audio Acrobat: www.audioacrobat.com
Audiopodium: www.imagobyphone.com/audio_podium.html
BYO Audio: www.byoaudio.com
Free Conference: www.freeconference.com
Free Conference Call: www.freeconferencecall.com
Mr. Conference Recordings: www.mrconferencerecordings.com
Phone Brain: www.phonebrain.com

Recording/Editing Software

Mac:
Audacity: audacity.sourceforge.net
Audio Hijack (recording): www.rogueamoeba.com/audiohijack/
Fission (editing): www.rogueamoeba.com/fission/
Garageband (part of iLife): www.apple.com/ilife/garageband/
Record Pad Sound Recording:
  www.nch.com.au/recordpad/index.html
Toast: www.roxio.com/enu/products/toast/default.html
Wave Pad Sound Editor: www.nch.com.au/wavepad/index.html

PC:

Adobe Audition: www.adobe.com/products/audition/main.html

Dak 2000:   www.dak2000.com/Reviews/2050story.cfm

Gold Wave: www.goldwave.com

Record Pad Sound Recording:
     www.nch.com.au/recordpad/index.html

Sony Jam Trax: www.sonycreativesoftware.com/jamtrax

Sony Sound Forge Audio Studio:
     www.sonycreativesoftware.com/audiostudio

Total Recorder: www.highcriteria.com

Wave Pad Sound Editor: www.nch.com.au/wavepad/index.html

Recording Equipment, Packaging and Supplies

Radio Shack: www.radioshack.com

Digital Loggers Digital Call Recorder (PC):
     www.digitalloggers.com/dli.personal.html

Cam Audio: www.camaudio.com

See Resources for chapter 8 for additional suggestions.

VIDEO

Webcams and Camcorders

Microsoft Lifecam

Logitech Quickcam

Apple iSight (has built-in software)

Any digital camcorder

Video Recording Software

Open Video Capture:
     www.008soft.com/products/video-capture.htm

Super Webcam Recorder:
     www.free-screen-capture.com/webcam-recorder-capture/

Video Editing Software

Final Cut Express: www.apple.com/finalcutexpress
Final Cut Studio: www.apple.com/finalcutstudio
Apple iMovie: www.apple.com/ilife/imovie
Apple iDVD: www.apple.com/ilife/idvd

Video Recording Service

Audio Acrobat: www.audioacrobat.com

AUDIO AND VIDEO

Duplication and Packaging

ADR: www.adrbookprint.com/Flash.html
Cam Audio: www.camaudio.com
Digital Excellence: www.digx.com
eDocPublish: www.edocpublish.com
OneDisc: www.onedisc.com

TWELVE

SPEAKING AND WORKSHOPS

Getting in front of an audience is one of the best ways to connect with potential clients and attract them into your coaching practice.

You may be interested in speaking or doing workshops for their own sake—because you love being in front of an audience and teaching. In this chapter, we'll approach this topic with respect to using it as a marketing tool.

BENEFITS

◆ **Give clients a live experience of you**

People hire a coach they connect with personally. Speaking and workshops are the best way to show potential clients who you are and what you can do for them.

◆ **Demonstrate your expertise**

During your speaking engagement, you can talk about clients you've worked with and share their success stories—how they benefited from working with you — as well as demonstrating a coaching conversation and processes or exercises that you work with.

◆ **Develop your materials and programs**

During your workshops, you can test out new processes and materials that you'd like to work with. If you're writing a book, you can test-drive the materials in your workshops, so that you can get hands-on experience and feedback to fine-tune your content, gather case studies and be able to write about it from a place of actual experience, and not just theory or speculation.

◆ **Connect personally with potential clients**

Some individuals will want to connect with you one-on-one before they sign up for coaching. After your talk, you can stick around, answer questions and even schedule appointments.

◆ **Gather information to follow up with interested attendees**

Have your attendees fill out an interest survey, or collect their business cards to raffle off a book or coaching session. This gives you the information — and an excuse — to follow up with them after the event.

◆ **Give special offers or discounts**

You can use your personal appearances as an opportunity to offer a special discount to anyone present who signs up for coaching. To create some urgency, it's best to put a time limit on your offer — for example: Sign up tonight (or within a certain number of days) and get 25% off your first month.

◆ **Additional income stream**

Teaching and speaking can provide another stream of income. You can offer entry-level workshops, as well as advanced classes and coaching groups. As you become more proficient and in demand as a speaker, you can begin commanding fees for your appearances. Serious speakers can sign up with the National Speakers Association (www.nsaspeaker.org) or seek out a speakers' bureau that books engagements for you.

♦ **Coordinate with your books and audio/video products**

Having a book can be an entrée into speaking opportunities, and having a presence in the public eye (your "platform") can lead to a book contract.

GETTING STARTED

Purpose of Your Talk or Workshop

Begin by defining what you want to accomplish by doing your talk or workshop.

♦ **Marketing**

As I mentioned above, public appearances are the best way to market your coaching practice. Potential clients not only get a personal experience of you, but prospects who don't attend your event may see your name in the advertisement or catalog (which gives you additional credibility) and contact you.

♦ **For its own sake**

Perhaps there's a message that you want to get out there or a skill that you want to teach. For example, my passion is to help people get into careers and jobs they love. I do that with individual clients, but I also express that purpose through teaching and writing.

• **Group coaching**

As an adjunct to working with individuals, you may also want to offer group coaching. This offers clients the additional support of the group, as well as a lower price-point item for those who can't afford one-on-one coaching.

What If I Want to Speak, But I'm Afraid

Reportedly, public speaking is one of our greatest fears. If getting in front of an audience terrifies you, then work with some of the other tools in this book. You have many choices; there's no need to suffer.

If you're afraid, but motivated to work through the fear, then work with the process in this chapter to build your skill and confidence.

Learning to Be a Teacher or Speaker

If you're new to teaching or speaking, you'll need to work on your skills. Here are some ways to do that.

◆ **Take classes and read books**

If you like a structured, academic approach, look online and at local continuing education programs for classes on teaching and training. For a time-tested, structured program, join a local Toastmasters group. You can also find numerous books on speaking, training and adult learning and development.

◆ **Observe other workshop leaders and speakers**

If you like to teach, you probably also like to attend workshops and seminars. When you do, notice what the teacher is doing and what you like and don't like about their approach and their content. Do you like their manner (e.g., professional, academic, friendly, funny)? Do they mostly lecture, or do they use a lot of interactivity? Do they include visuals or handouts? Start formulating your own approach, using this information to guide you.

◆ **Work with a mentor**

Some people learn best through customized, one-on-one instruction from a mentor. To find a mentor, approach someone you know and admire, attend a National Speakers Association meeting or search online for a presentation or speakers' coach.

◆ **Start small**

Don't feel you need to aim for being a keynote speaker at a major conference. Start slowly and build your skill and the size audience you feel comfortable handling. You might want to begin by working with a partner, where you share in both writing and presenting the workshop. Another easy start is to do teleclasses, where you can sit with your notes in front of you.

◆ **Start someplace comfortable**

Do your first workshops or talks in places where you feel at home. You might invite a few friends and do a presentation in your living room. Look for speaking opportunities with groups you already belong to, where you know people and feel supported. I live in a large apartment complex, and I did my first workshops (with a teaching partner) in the community room right downstairs, with some of my friends and neighbors attending. Later on, I did presentations at networking groups I regularly attended. (See chapter 15 for more on networking.)

Presentation Formats

Your presentations can take on different sizes and formats.

◆ **Talks or speaking engagements**

Your speaking engagements can be short presentations or longer keynotes (usually reserved for more experienced speakers). Many community groups and professional associations bring in speakers. At conferences, you can offer a "breakout" or "concurrent" session, which can be anywhere from 45 minutes to two hours. These may be a combination talk/workshop.

◆ **Workshops**

Workshops generally engage the group more than talks — people come to learn a skill or information. Workshops may be one-time (e.g., an evening or full day) or a series (e.g., a weekend workshop or one that meets weekly for several sessions).

◆ **Ongoing coaching groups**

A coaching group may meet weekly, biweekly or monthly, depending on the intensity of the work the group participants are doing. Groups that meet less often than monthly tend to lose momentum and connection.

Defining Topics

As always, if you're using your speaking engagement or workshop to bring clients into your coaching practice, you want to choose topics that speak to your target audience and support your brand.

Here are some directions to look when exploring possible topics:

◆ **What will interest your target audience?**

Begin by looking at the topics and issues on which you're typically coaching your clients. What issues come up for them? What skills or information would be helpful to them?

You might do a "needs analysis" by creating a survey or researching trends. Look at what people want vs. what you think they need. Coaches tend to be on the visionary edge, and your audience might not be ready for the fabulous cutting-edge material that you love. Some people may not be ready to confront issues head-on and need to ease into the topic. Meet them where they are.

◆ **Where do you have expertise and experience?**

Your professional and personal experience gives you insights that you can share and credibility to help your audience trust you. What knowledge or skill do you have that will be of interest to your target audience?

◆ **What materials would you like to develop?**

One of the coolest things about coaching is that we can use our own growth to benefit our clients. In what way would *you* like to develop? One coach I know revamps his practice every few years, depending on what he's interested in learning about at the time.

Is there a new concept that you would like to learn more about? A coaching program you'd like to develop? Would you like to test out material for a book? Shape your materials so you can try them out, but also make sure that your audience benefits from your learning experience.

◆ **What would you enjoy teaching?**

What are you passionate about? What have you learned or experienced that you'd like to teach? What challenges have you successfully navigated, where you have resources and strategies that you would like to share with others facing that challenge?

While many of my workshops have been about career and publishing — areas where I have professional training and experience — I've also done workshops on "Making Powerful Choices," a subject I've explored extensively for my own benefit, and "Being a Tortoise in a World of Hares™," a concept that evolved out of my own frustration at being an ambitious, but energy-challenged person and the strategies I've developed to help myself feel accomplished and productive.

◆ **What is the market calling for?**

While you may have great ideas about what you want to teach or speak about, will they sell to your target market? Is the market already glutted around this topic?

If your key topic is already being covered, there are two things you can do: 1) be creative and find a unique approach, and 2) find a different venue — a different library or learning center or organization where that topic is not yet being taught.

Also, look for new topics that are current, and perhaps urgent concerns for your target audience.

Creating a Compelling Title

One of the best ways to get someone into your workshop is to have a compelling title. You can even "recycle" material you've used before under a new title, rather than writing each workshop from scratch.

EXERCISE 1
Exploring Workshop Titles

Get one or more catalogs from adult learning centers or continuing education programs in your area. Look at the course titles. What catches your eye? Which ones are the most intriguing? What do you like about them? Which ones feel flat and boring? Would you be drawn to the class if it had a catchier title?

EXERCISE 2
Workshop Ideas

Brainstorm ideas for workshops you could teach or talks you could give that would appeal to your target audience. Make a list of 10 to 25 titles or topic ideas that you could speak about or teach.

❧

What Makes a Talk or Workshop Interesting?

As you begin putting together your talk or workshop, consider including the following components.

◆ **Interactivity**

The more people are involved, personally experiencing what you're teaching, the more likely they'll want to work with you privately. Even in a talk, find ways to involve the audience by asking questions where they can respond by raising their hand (e.g., How many of you . . . ?) or writing their response in a notebook. Do exercises where they can interact with the person sitting next to them or a small group.

◆ **Include success stories or case studies**

Stories make your presentation more interesting, beyond just sharing information. They show your audience exactly how you were able to help your clients by applying that information and what the result was. Many people are nervous about spending the big bucks to hire a coach, when they have no idea what to expect. Stories illustrate that coaching does, indeed, work and what can be achieved by working with you.

◆ **Humor**

People learn better when they're having fun. I think back to the required history class I took in college where I (generally an A student) got a C: The teaching was dry and boring, and the most engaging thing in the class was the chocolate tobacco my classmate smoked. Using appropriate humor keeps people entertained and engaged, and they're more likely to remember what you said.

◆ **Relevance to your audience**

Your audience needs to be able to relate to what you're saying. If you're giving a talk for a particular group, find out what their concerns and interests are.

◆ **Focus**

It's important to stay on topic and not wander off in different directions. People appreciate a talk or workshop that has a beginning, middle and end. It should have the optimal amount of content: If it's too much, people will feel overwhelmed; if it's too little, they'll feel cheated. You want to give them something of value that feels complete, but leaves the door open for doing additional work with you.

HOW TO WORK WITH SPEAKING AND WORKSHOPS

Now that you've considered topics and titles, and what will make your presentation more compelling, let's move ahead with the next steps.

Putting It Together

You'll need to write your speech or workshop. You may want to come up with a detailed script or just a structure with talking points, from which you can speak extemporaneously.

Here are some things to think about when putting together your presentation.

◆ **Start with what you know**

I'm assuming that the topic you've chosen is something you know at least a little bit about. Begin by listing the key points you would like to cover. Think of the flow, and begin to give it some structure — a beginning, middle and end. Then, write down information relevant to each point that you would like to include.

EXERCISE
Creating an Outline

Create a preliminary outline for your presentation. Write down the key points you would like to cover. Put them in a logical order. Write down next to each point anything that you currently know you would like to say about that topic. For a workshop, include any exercises or activities you would like to include.

Remember — this is not set in stone. It's only a beginning point from which you can flesh out your talk or workshop.

❧

◆ **Research**

Use research to add to what you already know. Find books, search the Internet, take classes or interview experts who can add additional perspectives to the topic. (Tip: When using information from the Internet, be sure to check the validity. Anybody can post anything on the Internet, true or not.)

◆ **Make it interactive and experiential**

Get variety in the class by alternating lecture with experiential processes. People learn by repetition and experience. Use exercises and worksheets to reinforce the learning. From a marketing perspective, people are more likely to call you for coaching if they've had a personal breakthrough or insight, rather than just gathering data.

Use the wisdom of the participants. People in the class can learn from each other, not just you. Include exercises where the students work in pairs or small groups, and then have them share their small-group experience with the whole class. Even in a large group, you can have them interact with small groups within the class.

There are also ways you can interact with your audience in a talk. I was in a seminar with Martha Beck and saw her use a brilliant technique: To illustrate the process she was teaching, she selected four people to interact with and took them through the steps of the process. This created a thread through the seminar and a live experience that we could all witness.

◆ **Make it concise and focused**

If you're using your workshop as a marketing tool, you don't want to give it all away. Give something of value, that's complete in itself, but that leaves the door open to work with you individually to take it to the next level.

You also don't want to overload your audience. You don't have to throw in the kitchen sink to give them their money's worth —

especially if they're only paying $50! A professional training, where participants are paying top dollar to learn something, is different.

For a workshop that you're using as a low-priced marketing tool, choose one focus, then explore and reinforce it. It's better to do one thing fully than overload your audience with more information than they can take in. You want to leave them feeling excited and enthusiastic, not discouraged and overwhelmed.

◆ Make it fun

As I said above, humor promotes learning by reducing stress and seriousness. This is not about getting up there and doing a stand-up comedy routine. Find humor that's relevant to your topic and integrates with your presentation — anecdotes and stories that illustrate your concepts, or what not to do!

Also, people are more likely to pursue coaching with you if they feel it's going to be an enjoyable experience, rather than a grueling, serious one.

EXERCISE
Developing Your Workshop

Using the points above, as well as the rest of this chapter, continue developing your outline into a complete talk or workshop. As with any writing project, do it in several sittings, allowing the material and structure to evolve.

◆ Include some visuals

Some people learn best, and find it easier to focus their attention, when there's a visual component. It can be high-tech or low-tech — anything from paper handouts to PowerPoint slides to an animated on-screen presentation. Just make sure that your visuals don't overshadow your verbal presentation.

PowerPoint Guidelines

One of the most popular ways to present visuals is by using PowerPoint slides. Here are a few guidelines to make sure that your visuals enhance your presentation, rather than detracting from it.

◆ **Don't overdo it**

Limit your slides to 20 to 30 per one-hour presentation.

◆ **Keep it simple**

Include only key points. Use short phrases and bullet points that can be read quickly, so attendees are not reading your slides when they should be listening to you.

◆ **Make it legible**

Make sure your type is big enough to be read at the back of the room. Text should be at least 24 point and titles 36 point type. Use no more than two fonts (you might use one for text and one for titles, one **serif** and one **sans serif**).

Include adequate space between the lines. If you have a lot of information, split it into two or more slides. Don't try to squish it all on one page.

When choosing colors, make sure you have good contrast between the text and the background.

◆ **Don't compete with your visuals**

If you're showing a film clip or an illustration, bring up the slide and pause to give your audience time to take it in before you continue speaking.

◆ **Use graphics effectively**

If you can, get your message across with a graphic. It's easier for a viewer to take in a picture along with your spoken words, rather than trying to read and listen at the same time. Graphics can be fun and appealing, but be careful not to overdo special effects that distract from your presentation.

♦ **Include only what you're covering**

Your slides should coordinate with your presentation. Don't include slides that are not relevant to what you're covering. When you skip over them, it leaves your audience feeling they're missing out on something. If you have multiple variations of your presentation, have a different PowerPoint file for each version.

• **Distribute handouts at the end**

PowerPoint can generate beautiful handouts from your presentation slides. Unless you want participants to take notes right on the handouts, save them till the end. You don't want your audience shuffling papers when their attention should be on you. Let them know ahead of time that handouts will be distributed later, so they don't feel they need to write down material that's already on the slides.

Content and Structure

Now, you're ready to start putting together your speech or workshop. Here are some suggestions.

Talk or Speech

A talk or speech can run anywhere from 30 minutes to two hours. As a speaker, you're both informing and entertaining your audience.

♦ **Choose one main focus**

A talk is generally too short to cover a range of topics without overwhelming your audience. Choose one focus and give it appropriate coverage for the allotted time.

◆ **Have a beginning, middle and end**

A common structure for a talk is to tell them what you're going to tell them, tell them, then review what you told them. Whatever topic you choose to cover, whatever level of depth, make sure the presentation feels complete. While you do want to leave them wanting more, you don't want them to feel cheated, especially if they paid to hear you.

Leaving out the ending because you ran out of time leaves people feeling frustrated. I once attended a teleseminar on the "Top Ten Ways" to do something. We only covered six ways, and it left me feeling angry with the presenter for not giving what he promised.

◆ **Include stories / case studies / humor**

Give examples that demonstrate what you do, as well as success stories. People want to know: What can you do for me? This is how you show them. Stories also help to clarify and flesh out your data, so that your audience can understand and relate to it in a more personal way. Including some humor keeps your audience engaged.

◆ **Include the audience**

Even with a large group, you can get your audience involved by asking questions that they can respond to by a show of hands. Hand out simple worksheets that they can do in a few minutes, or have them explore a question with a partner. If it's appropriate, you can invite people to share their learning with the full group.

◆ **Don't make it one long sales pitch**

Yes, you're using your talk to promote your coaching business. But if your audience perceives that it's just a sales pitch, and you're not giving them anything of value, they'll turn off.

EXERCISE
Structuring My Talk

Use the following points to begin structuring your talk.

- Topic and title

- What I want my audience to walk away with

- Key talking points

- Stories and examples that support my talking points

- Ways I can include my audience (questions, worksheets, exercises, demonstrations)

Workshop

People come to workshops to learn new information or skills, in more depth than they would get from a talk. A workshop may run for two to four hours, a full day, a weekend or several days spread over weeks or months.

Following is a basic structure that works well.

- **Introductions**

  Introductions make the workshop more personal and get people engaged. When they know who their fellow students are, they're more likely to open up and participate.

  If the group is small enough, and you have the time, have each person share their name, what brought them to the workshop, and perhaps the answer to a relevant questions, such as, What's one question you would like to have answered as a result of doing this workshop?

  If the group is large, have each person introduce themselves to three or four of their neighbors. Also, introduce yourself and give some of your background, particularly citing what qualifies you to teach this class.

♦ **Agenda or course objectives**

People feel more comfortable when they know what to expect. Either have a printed agenda and/or course objectives, or state them at the beginning of the class. Let participants know how the session will run, if and when they can expect breaks and the logistics of the workshop venue. You can cover this either before or after the introductions.

♦ **Guidelines**

Also set up expectations for the behavior you expect. If there will be participation, set parameters to create a safe space. You might let them know you expect confidentiality around anything that's shared; ask them to embrace each person's ideas; and set up any other behavior that will create safety for participants and encourage them to engage freely with the exercises.

♦ **Warm-up exercise or discussion**

Very often, people are coming to your workshop early in the morning, when they're still groggy, or after work, when they're tired. Start with a simple exercise or discussion to get people present and focused on the topic of the workshop. There are books of these "icebreakers" available.

♦ **Philosophy**

Give some background information or philosophy about your topic to create a context for the learning. For example, when I did a workshop on Finding Work You Love, I talked about Maslow's hierarchy of needs and how that relates to finding work that's meaningful and fulfilling, rather than working just to take care of your survival needs.

This can be a lecture or an interactive discussion. It's also a good place to include stories and case histories.

◆ **Interactive exercises**

Next, you'll get your students involved by doing exercises. These might be paper-and-pencil exercises or interactive ones, which might be verbal or also include movement. One strategy is to demonstrate the exercise with one student (or a co-presenter), and then have the class break into pairs or small groups and do it themselves.

This is an opportunity to demonstrate what you do as a coach. When people have an enjoyable experience, along with insights and breakthroughs, it can encourage them to seek you out for additional, one-on-one coaching to accelerate their progress.

◆ **Sharing**

After each exercise, "debrief" by having participants share what they learned or experienced. This solidifies the learning and allows students to learn from each other. If the exercise was done with the full group, have them share with the group or a partner. If the exercise was done with a partner or small group, have them share their insights with the full group. You can have them share after each exercise or after a related series of exercises.

◆ **Repeat the last three steps**

If your workshop is long enough, you'll run through the last three steps several times. Alternating philosophy and interaction, and going back and forth between partners and the full group, brings more variety and keeps participants from "spacing out" during long lectures.

◆ **Optional material**

Different groups will go through the material at different paces. Create some flexibility for yourself by including extra, optional material to use if you need it, as well as material that you can omit if the workshop runs late. Make sure that the workshop is still complete if you don't get to it.

◆ **Plan of Action**

Coaching is about action, so we want to leave people with an action step, to make it more than just an interesting interlude. Even if your workshop is short, have participants come up with one or two steps they can take based on what they learned. If the workshop is several sessions, do an action plan at the end of each session and hold students accountable for steps they agreed to take.

◆ **Feedback or interest form**

At the end of your workshop — whatever the length — use a feedback or interest form to collect contact information and find out what types of coaching or other workshops participants might be interested in. (For a multi-session workshop, you'll collect contact information at the first session, if you don't already have it from registration.) This is also an opportunity to collect names for your mailing list by having them sign up for your free e-newsletter (see chapter 6).

Keep your feedback form short and simple — by the end of a workshop, people are often tired and eager to leave. You might use a checklist that includes the types of coaching you do and other workshops you offer. To collect feedback anonymously — and possibly get more honest responses — use a stamped, self-addressed postcard or an online service such as SurveyMonkey.com.

◆ **Completion**

Bring closure to the workshop by opening the floor to sharing (perhaps sharing what they got from the workshop or the action they want to take), doing a guided meditation or raffling off a relevant gift (such as your book or CD or a coaching session). A raffle is also a great way to collect contact information — have each person drop a business card in a bowl at the beginning of the class.

EXERCISE
Structuring My Workshop

Use the following points to begin structuring your workshop.

◆ Topic and title

◆ Agenda and guidelines for the class

◆ What I want my audience to walk away with

◆ Key talking points

◆ Exercises and processes I can do

◆ Stories that support my talking points

◆ For a multi-session workshop, homework assignments

◆ How I want to close the workshop

Workshop Proposal

When you're beginning to teach, or working with a new venue, you'll generally need to submit a written proposal to your prospective workshop sponsor. Once they know you, very often you can just submit new ideas with a brief description and/or write the catalog copy for your workshop.

Here are some of the components to include in your proposal.

◆ **Course description / outline**

In paragraph form or using bullet points, explain what your workshop is about. Include enough detail to adequately describe your class, but don't overdo it. Make it easy for a busy person to take in. It helps to write your description in a compelling way. If you need help with that, hire a writer or editor, or pick up a book on writing advertising copy.

◆ **Course objectives**

Sponsors want to know what your students can expect to gain from taking your course. This may be new knowledge, skills, insights or personal or professional advancement. Be specific and appropriate to your sponsoring organization. "Feel more connected to their inner selves" may fly in some venues, but sound flaky in others.

◆ **Your biography**

Include your professional history, credentials and anything else that makes you the perfect person to teach this course.

◆ **Catalog or flyer copy**

If you have access to your sponsor's catalog or previous flyers, write the copy for them! The easier you can make their job, and fit in with their way of doing things, the better they'll like it and continue to book your workshops.

◆ **Cover letter**

Include a short, compelling cover letter that will persuade your prospective sponsor to continue and read the core of your proposal.

See appendix C for a sample workshop proposal.

Where to Present

In looking for places to speak or do your workshop, you'll want to find venues that attract your ideal client. Depending on your target audience, look at some of the following:

◆ Adult learning centers — Depending on your location, look for places such as the Learning Annex, the local Y, community colleges, libraries and continuing education programs.

- Places where people are into personal growth — Consider health clubs, spas, retreat centers, spiritual centers, health food stores and bookstores that feature self-help sections.

- Association meetings — These professional groups are always looking for speakers on business or personal topics (such as stress management, work/life balance or how to dress for success) that their members will benefit from. Find associations related to your target audience in the phone book or on the Internet, or go to the library and find a directory of associations.

- Industry conferences — Conferences and conventions are always looking for speakers to do keynote and breakout (aka, "concurrent") sessions. Look for conferences that attract your target group.

- Special interest groups — Find groups that attract your audience, such as entrepreneurial groups, young professionals, parenting groups, spiritual groups, or personal growth support groups or classes.

While you'll get the most interest in coaching when you target both the topics of your presentations and your audiences, when you're just beginning, you might want to present to any interested audience that you can in order to gain experience.

When you work with a sponsoring organization, they will generally advertise and provide a space for your talk or workshop. If you're doing it on your own, you'll need to foot the expenses and take on the risk yourself.

Research spaces that are appropriate for your type of workshop and fit your budget. Seek out advertising venues that will reach more of your target audience and give you more bang for your buck. Unless your topic is a very popular one and you can expect a large number of people for a nominal fee, you may want to target a select group that's willing to pay a higher price to get the value of your workshop. You will, of course, need to provide that value.

What's Your Comfort Level?

When you're strategizing your teaching plan, take into account your comfort level with different types of teaching. If you're just beginning, consider some of these options:

- Start with a phone class (aka, "teleclass"). It allows you to keep your notes in front of you and practice your material.

- Start with a small group, possibly one where you know people and feel comfortable with them, such as a professional or community group you belong to. You might even invite a group of friends to your home to test out some material and get feedback. You may find you most enjoy working with these small, intimate groups. If you want, work your way up to mid-size and large groups.

- Work with a partner. Find someone with common goals and interests. Work together to write your workshop, and then present it together. Take turns presenting parts of the workshop, so each of you has time to sit back and observe, without having to carry the entire workshop yourself.

As you grow in skill and comfort, you can expand your list of topics, the length of your workshops and the size of the groups you work with. You may continue working with a partner or "go solo," as you get more comfortable in front of an audience and build your stamina for doing longer workshops.

When You Get There

As you're preparing your workshop, create a checklist of things you need to bring, so you don't forget anything in the last-minute flurry. See appendix D for a sample checklist.

On the day of the workshop, arrive early. Give yourself plenty of time to set up and get the lay of the land, so you don't feel rushed.

- Arrange the room. If you have flexibility, set it up so that your attendees will be most comfortable. If you have a small group, you may want to move the chairs into a semi-circle to promote rapport and comfort in sharing.

◆ Set up any technology that you'll be using. Test it! If someone else set it up, don't assume it will work. Test it yourself, and make sure you know how to use the equipment.

◆ Prepare your handouts and materials. Put handouts on the seats, or set them up to be distributed at the beginning or end of the presentation. Put your business cards, brochures and flyers where students can pick them up as they enter. If you'll be selling products, set up a table for them.

◆ Be present. As your students come in, be available to greet them and answer questions. As you begin the presentation, set the tone. Do you want it to be formal and business-like? Warm and friendly? Model the tone and the behavior you expect.

◆ Deliver what you promised. If you advertised that you will cover "The Top Ten Ways to …," make sure you cover all ten ways. Stick to your agenda and time frame. People don't appreciate running overtime at the end of a long day, especially if they have a subsequent commitment.

Follow-Up Marketing

To make your presentation an effective marketing tool, you need to follow up with interested participants. Here are some ways to do that.

◆ Hand out business cards, brochures, flyers or one-sheets (see chapter 13) to promote your services, products and any upcoming workshops, and make sure participants know how to contact you.

◆ Collect contact information. Some of the ways to do that:
  – Collect business cards and raffle off a product or coaching session
  – Have participants complete a feedback form that includes a checklist of the types of coaching you offer, as well as other workshops you offer that may interest them

  – Have people sign up to subscribe to your newsletter or mailing
    list to stay informed of future events

◆ Be available to answer questions after the presentation. Some
  people need to connect with you personally to feel comfortable
  signing on for coaching.

◆ Offer a time-limited discount if they sign up on the spot or within
  a designated time frame (e.g., with a week) for a follow-up session
  or to begin a coaching engagement.

◆ Sell products. Books, audios and videos can be the next level of
  entry, where potential clients can get to know you better and gain
  the confidence that will encourage them to take the next step and
  pursue coaching with you. (See chapters 10 and 11.)

Other Formats

Aside from typical workshops and speaking engagements, there are
several other ways to present your material and get in front of
audiences.

Proprietary Coaching Programs

Some coaches are developing and trademarking coaching programs.
They use these with clients, and also train and license other coaches
to work with their system.

If you've put together a unique coaching strategy, you might
consider trademarking the name and copyrighting the material and
offering it to others via workshops, books and audios.

Group Coaching

Some coaches enjoy working with groups. You may form a group
around a particular focus, such as career, small business or parenting,
or have it be a general coaching group, open to a variety of focuses.
Groups also offer another entry-level product, with a lower price

point than individual coaching. Some group members may want more personal attention and shift to working with you one-on-one.

Teleclasses or Teleseminars

These classes, given over the phone via a "bridge line," may be offered for free, to attract potential clients, or for a fee, as an income stream in themselves. You may offer single classes, where you touch on different topics as "teasers" (perhaps linking them together as a series), or do a multi-session class, where you offer more in-depth material.

Teleclasses generally run an hour, and not more than two hours — any longer than that and people lose focus, and it's hard to give a break when you're on the phone! The advantage of working by phone is that you can reach people anywhere, not just in your local area. It's also a great way to demonstrate the effectiveness of coaching over the phone for those who are skeptical.

You can list your teleclass at Teleclass.com, as well as advertising it through your website and your other marketing outlets. See the Resources section for some places where you can get access to free bridge lines.

Webinars

You can present a web-based seminar or use online visuals to enhance a teleseminar. This is great for people who learn visually, and more dynamic than a paper or PDF handout.

E-mail Self-Study Programs

An approach that ultimately demands less of your time is to develop a virtual self-study course that's disseminated through a series of e-mails, often set up as timed autoresponders on a shopping cart system. Once a student signs up, the lessons are distributed automatically, such as one a week. In each e-mail, you would provide some content and an assignment that students can do on their own.

Because these programs are automated, once the up-front work is done, they become a source of passive income. You can also package the program with optional one-on-one coaching for a higher fee.

Packaged Learning Programs

These programs include various components, such as workbooks, DVDs, audio CDs and data CDs, which might include such things as worksheets or PowerPoint presentations. These tangible products require order fulfillment and shipping, so they're not as automatic as e-mail programs, but they are another source of passive income once they're created.(See chapter 10 for creating books and e-books and chapter 11 for creating audios and videos.)

RESOURCES

The following resources are offered as suggestions, and NOT recommendations. Internet businesses in particular are notorious for changing. If you are considering using any of these vendors, check them out carefully and make an informed decision.

Books

Speak Without Fear: A Total System for Becoming a Natural, Confident Communicator, by Ivy Naistadt

Secrets of Successful Speakers: How You Can Motivate, Captivate, and Persuade, by Lilly Walters

The Elements of Speechwriting and Public Speaking, by Jeff Scott Cook

The Lost Art of the Great Speech: How to Write One—How to Deliver It, by Richard Dowis

Designing Effective Workshops & Teleclasses, by Karyn Greenstreet

Workshops: Designing and Facilitating Experiential Learning, by Jeff E. Brooks-Harris and Susan R. Stock-Ward

Learning to Listen, Learning to Teach: The Power of Dialogue in Educating Adults, by Jane Vella

The Complete Guide to Facilitation: Enabling Groups to Succeed, by Tom Justice and David Jamieson

The Secrets of Facilitation: The S.M.A.R.T. Guide to Getting Results With Groups, by Michael Wilkinson

For additional resources, go to Amazon.com and other online bookstores and do keyword searches on:

- Public speaking
- Facilitation
- Teaching
- Speechwriting
- Presentations
- Adult learning

Speaker Training

Toastmasters International: www.toastmasters.org

American Speaker Training Camp: www.speakertrainingcamp.com

Media Training Worldwide:
www.mediatrainingworldwide.com/speaker-training.html

Speakers Bureaus and Associations

National Speakers Association: www.nsaspeaker.org

NSA has a referral service for members. To find additional speakers bureaus, do an online search for "speakers bureau." Be sure to check out any organization with which you're considering affiliating.

Teleclasses

Teleclass.com: www.teleclass.net

Bridge (Conferencing) Lines

Eagle Teleconferencing: www.eagletel.com
Free Conference: www.freeconference.com
Free Conference Call: www.freeconferencecall.com
TeleConferenceLine: www.teleconferenceline.com

Webinars and Web Conferencing

Communique: www.communiqueconferencing.com/webinar.asp
Go To Meeting: www.gotomeeting.com
Go To Webinar: www.gotowebinar.com
MetaMeeting: www.megameeting.com
Webex: www.webex.com

Space to Rent

Eventective: www.eventective.com

Section III:
OTHER WAYS TO MARKET

THIRTEEN

PROMOTIONAL MATERIALS

While a great deal of marketing has "gone virtual," there are still some printed materials that are beneficial to have. These may include business cards, letterhead and envelopes, brochures, flyers, one-sheets and postcards (aka, "pushcards"). You may also want to have some promotional giveaway items.

BENEFITS

♦ **Gives you credibility**

Along with your website, having printed materials gives you professional credibility. Writing your name and phone number on a scrap of paper just doesn't make the same impression as a printed business card.

♦ **Have something to leave behind when you meet people**

You definitely want to have a business card, and possibly a brochure or postcard, for networking and casual meetings. People are impulse buyers (not to mention overwhelmed), and if they have to remember your name and look you up on the Internet, there's a good chance they'll forget.

- **Have something to send people to introduce yourself and your services**

  If you're looking to court referral sources or create business alliances and opportunities (see chapter 16), sending nice-looking, well-written information materials can make a good first impression. This is particularly important if you're selling to businesses.

- **Use for follow-up**

  Once you've made a connection with a prospect, printed materials are a great way to follow up. With so many people communicating virtually, printed communications sent by "snail mail" get noticed. You can reinforce a face-to-face meeting with a letter on nice stationery, and perhaps include a brochure or coupon.

- **Offer a useful item that keeps your name in front of your prospect**

  A promotional item, such as a pen or calendar that someone will use, keeps your name in front of them for a year or more.

GETTING STARTED

Begin by considering which materials you'll need. I would say a definite "yes" on business cards and stationery. If you need a "leave-behind," consider whether a trifold brochure, one-sheet, postcard or pushcard or some other format represents you best. If you're seriously pursuing a speaking career, a one-sheet is mandatory. If you want to make your leave-behind a little more memorable, consider a pen, calendar, keychain or a pad of sticky notes with your name, your business name and contact information.

If you're already working with a Web designer, find out whether they can use the same logo, colors and graphics to create printed materials for you. Have them send you the digital graphics files, so you can insert your logo on faxes and for your e-mail signature. If you're adept with graphics, you may be able to set these up yourself.

HOW TO WORK WITH PROMOTIONAL MATERIALS

Creating Your "Corporate Identity"

In today's world of advertising "noise," you need to create a unique brand or identity for your business to get noticed. In the "olden days," your business card and stationery created your business identity. It still does, along with your website and other tangible and virtual materials.

Even though a lot of business is conducted virtually, you still need a business card for networking and chance meetings, so you have something to hand to prospects, as well as letterhead and envelopes for the occasional business letter you may need to send. You can also use your letterhead to create fax cover sheets and client forms.

When you're just beginning, you can get inexpensive stationery and business cards, either locally or from online sources such as Vistaprint.com or iPrint.com. As you become more established, it's advisable to create a unique identity. Hire a graphic designer (possibly your Web designer) to create a logo and a "look" that you'll use on your virtual and printed materials.

If you're doing business or organizational coaching (which requires a slicker look) or want to go "high-end," have custom business cards and stationery commercially printed. If you rarely use printed communication, have your designer set up your letterhead and envelope as PDF documents. Invest in nice paper from the local stationery store or a vendor such as Paper Direct (see Resources), and print your letters and envelopes on your laser or inkjet printer. If your printer only prints in black, consider choosing a paper with color and/or texture.

Brochures and One-Sheets

While your website can contain vastly more information than a brochure or one-sheet (essentially, a flyer), these printed pieces can be useful as leave-behinds or promotional materials that you can make available when you do talks or workshops, or for your referral sources to leave in their waiting rooms (see chapter 16).

Your brochure may be a single page folded in half or a tri-fold. (Pre-scored brochure-weight paper is available from vendors such as Paper Direct.) A more elaborate piece might include several pages folded and stapled at the "spine." A one-sheet is just that—a single sheet, printed on one or both sides.

Some of the components you might include are:

◆ A brief explanation of coaching
◆ A brief description or bullet list of your services
◆ A list of the types of issues you typically work with or results you've achieved with clients
◆ A list of typical types of clients; for business coaching, you can list companies you've served
◆ A list of benefits clients get from working with you
◆ Testimonials
◆ A short bio or list of your credentials or qualifications
◆ Your picture
◆ Your logo
◆ Contact information

As with Web-based materials, be sure to incorporate your keywords—words and phrases with which your ideal clients can identify.

Other Formats

Additional formats you can use for leave-behinds or mailers include postcards (aka, "pushcards") and folded or unusually-shaped business cards. One unique format is a CD-ROM shaped as a business card, with the hole in the center. They're memorable, but they can be a little dicey to use, and generally won't run on a Macintosh.

Promotional Giveaways

You may also want to invest in promotional giveaways — useful items that include your business name and contact information. Common items are pens, calendars, totebags, t-shirts, mini-flashlights, mugs, mousepads, magnets and pads of sticky notes.

Café Press is an online vendor with a multitude of products to which you can add your own graphics. You can set up your own store and add a mark-up to each item, for an extra stream of passive income, or purchase the items at cost to use as giveaways.

You might also consider using e-documents or printed bookets as giveaways (see chapter 10).

RESOURCES

The following resources are offered as suggestions, and NOT recommendations. Internet businesses in particular are notorious for changing. If you are considering using any of these vendors, check them out carefully and make an informed decision.

Printing and Paper

Vistaprint: www.vistaprint.com
iPrint: www.iprint.com
Paper Direct: www.paperdirect.com
Staples: www.staples.com
Office Depot: www.officedepot.com

Promotional Items

Café Press: www.cafepress.com
Zazzle: www.zazzle.com

Do an Internet search on "promotional items."

Design Services

Guru: www.guru.com

Elance: www.elance.com

Creative Hot List: www.creativehotlist.com

Coroflot: www.coroflot.com

FOURTEEN

MEDIA

Getting your name and image in the media is a great way to put the word out to the general public about services and products you're offering and to enhance your visibility and credibility.

BENEFITS

◆ **Get your name in front of people**

Marketing is all about letting people know about you. With media appearances, your name becomes familiar, and potential clients are more likely to look you up and reach out to you.

◆ **Enhance your credibility**

Appearing in a magazine, newspaper, radio or TV show is a great way to build trust and value for your services and create name recognition. People feel that you've been sanctioned by the writer, publisher or host, and it adds to your professional credibility.

♦ **Establish you as an expert**

There's a perception that appearing in print or broadcast media makes you an expert. You can establish yourself as the "go-to" person for your area of expertise and encourage journalists to call *you* when they need a guest or a quote.

GETTING STARTED

Research Media Contacts

Begin by identifying appropriate media. If you're shy, you may want to stick to print media. If you're a great speaker and love an audience, go for radio and TV. Choose media that attract your target audience. For newspapers and magazines, target the specific sections or columns your prospects would read.

For print media, you're probably familiar with local newspapers and magazines, or you can look them up in the Yellow Pages or online. In large cities, different neighborhoods may each have their own small newspaper. If you want to expand your coverage, research national periodicals in a sourcebook such as the *Gale Directory of Publications and Broadcast Media*. This is an expensive set of volumes that's updated annually, so work with it in your public library.

For radio and TV, look in the Yellow Pages for local stations, search the Internet or consult the *Gale Directory* for national options. With cable and Internet, there are hundreds of radio and TV shows looking for guests. The beauty of radio is that you can usually call in from your home or office, so you're not limited to local stations. Even a small local appearance can get you noticed. Once, when I had appeared on a local cable TV show, several people mentioned to me that they had seen the program.

Another resource for radio and TV is the *Radio-TV Interview Report*, published by Bradley Communications (see Resources for this chapter). This publication is distributed free to radio and TV hosts who are looking for guests. As a potential guest, you would purchase half- or full-page ads, which can be run once or multiple times. If you choose to advertise, make sure you have a specific "hook" or area of expertise by which you can be identified.

If you want to write and submit your own articles, see chapter 9. To create your own videos for YouTube, see chapter 11.

EXERCISE
Media List

Make a list of media — magazines, newspapers, radio and TV shows — that would attract your target audience and that fit your style. Explore their websites and make note of important information, including:

- types of writers (to submit articles), interviewees or guests they feature
- writer or guest guidelines
- frequency of publication or airing
- submission guidelines and deadlines
- contact person and phone and/or e-mail

Buff Up Your Public Image

If you're going to actively seek public visibility, you want to begin by making sure that your own materials are up-to-date and represent the image you want to project.

- **Update your website**

   Be sure that all the information on your website is current. Update your biography, your events calendar and your coaching services. If you don't already have one, set up a Media or Press Room page, where you can include pictures, press releases and links to previous media you've done.

◆ **Clean up your Web presence**

It's also important to clean up your listings on LinkedIn, Facebook and any other websites on which you're listed. If you participate on any social media or blogs for fun, be careful not to post anything inflammatory that might come up on a Web search.

◆ **Get new headshots**

Your picture(s) should be current and professional. You might also want to have shots taken of you in action, e.g., speaking to a group, on the phone or coaching a client in your office.

EXERCISE
Public Image Checklist

Review the following to ensure that you're presented professionally:

❑ My website
❑ My social media
    ❑ LinkedIn
    ❑ Facebook
    ❑ MySpace
    ❑ _____
    ❑ _____
❑ Professional associations and other listings
    ❑ International Coach Federation
    ❑ _____
    ❑ _____
❑ Blogs on which I participate
    ❑ _____
    ❑ _____
❑ _____

HOW TO WORK WITH MEDIA

Begin by Being Proactive

When you begin working with media, you'll need to be *proactive*. While media coverage is free, you'll need to make time to reach out and establish yourself as a resource with reporters. In time, once you've created those relationships, they'll begin reaching out to you, and you can move into a *reactive* phase.

Prepare Your Materials

When you approach an interviewer or reporter, it's helpful to have the following materials available:

- **A bio and fact sheet**

  Include relevant information about yourself and your business, as well as topics that you can address as an expert.

- **Frequently asked questions**

  Reporters may not know the best questions to ask you. A FAQs page will stimulate ideas and give them reasons to contact you.

  Since most contact is virtual these days, have these available as PDFs that you can send as an e-mail attachment or that can be downloaded from the Media page on your website. These are generally sent *after* you make the initial contact with the reporter or host.

- **Perfect your pitch**

  Practice writing a compelling pitch that you can e-mail to contacts. It should be succinct (about 100 words) and tell a compelling story that sets you apart from others in your niche. The press particularly loves short pieces, such as steps or tips lists.

  See also the information on Press Kits and Press Releases on the following pages.

EXERCISE
Preparing Your Materials

1. Write your bio and fact sheet.
2. Write a list of FAQs.
3. Practice writing a pitch for a topic in which you are an expert.
4. Start putting together your press kit.

Make Yourself Valuable

In order to encourage reporters to contact you for quotes for their articles, or media hosts to invite you to be interviewed, you need to think of *their* perspective and bring value to their article or program.

◆ **Find a clear "hook" — an area of expertise for which interviewers can call on you**

In order to cut through all the advertising "noise," you need to be able to create a unique identity for yourself — that you're the best person to go to about this topic. Choose an area that correlates with your coaching focus, and go about becoming an expert.

◆ **Make it newsworthy**

While you may think your topic is fascinating, it also needs to appeal to the public. By making your topic newsworthy — or linking it to a current concern or trend — you're helping reporters do their job, and they're much more likely to call upon you for an interview or a quote.

Create Relationships

If you were looking for someone to interview, would you be more likely to call on someone who contacted you out of the blue or someone you knew and trusted? If you want to get regular media coverage, you need to invest in creating relationships with reporters and hosts.

Once you've made your media list, begin "courting" two or three at a time. Contact a specific person—sending something to a department (or no department at all) will probably doom it to the circular file. Introduce yourself with a call, e-mail or press kit. Let them know how you can be of value to them.

Once you've made a good connection, keep in touch (in a professional, non-pushy way) through occasional e-mails or press releases containing information that might be useful to them. Once they get to know you, they'll start calling you.

Press Kits and Press Releases

The professional way to approach media is through press releases and press kits.

Press Kits

Press kits are used to present yourself to potential media sources. A press kit may contain any of the following:

- An introductory cover letter
- A current press release (see below)
- A list of your area(s) of expertise and topics on which you can be interviewed
- A professional biography
- A professional photo
- Copies of press clippings or published articles
- A list of previous media appearances or interviews
- Promotional materials, such as a brochure or one-sheet (see chapter 13)
- Sample questions an interviewer can ask you
- Your business card
- A copy of your book

Press Releases

Press releases can be used to follow up with media contacts or on their own. Your releases need to be newsworthy. This may be the announcement of a new class, program or book that you've just released; a new company that you've formed; an upcoming media appearance; or how your work relates to a current hot topic. If you can link it to something that's in the news or trendy, so much the better.

By using the standard format for a press release, it's more likely to be taken seriously. This information is available in books and on the Web. See the Resources for this chapter for some links, and see appendix E for a sample.

EXERCISE
Write a Press Release

Following the format of the sample press release in appendix E, or one that you find in a book or online, craft a newsworthy press release for your coaching business.

Media Page

For additional coverage, you can post your press releases on a Media or Press Room page on your website. Along with listing previous mentions and appearances, this presents you as a credible and reliable news source. Even mentions in smaller periodicals, TV or radio shows or on lesser-known websites — especially if they include a link back to your website — can help get your name out there when journalists are searching for an expert to interview.

Your Media page can also include professional headshots and pictures of you speaking or on the air, a fact sheet or bio, press clippings, audio and video clips and a list of topics on which you have expertise.

Working with a Professional Publicist

If you really want to get serious about this, you might hire a publicist or public relations professional. To find one, ask your colleagues for recommendations, search the Internet (and, of course, check them out thoroughly) or track down the authors of books about public relations and publicity (see the Resources for this chapter for some ideas).

Getting Ready for Your Close-Up!

If you're planning on a serious media career, you may need to spiff yourself up a bit. You may want to do a makeover: get a new hairdo and wardrobe, train your voice or minimize that regional accent and practice being on-camera or using a microphone. See the Resources for this chapter for suggestions on finding appropriate professionals.

RESOURCES

The following resources are offered as suggestions, and NOT recommendations. Internet businesses in particular are notorious for changing. If you are considering using any of these vendors, check them out carefully and make an informed decision.

Books

Complete Publicity Plans: How to Create Publicity That Will Spark Media Exposure and Excitement, by Sandra L. Beckwith

Writing Effective News Releases...: How to Get Free Publicity for Yourself, Your Business, or Your Organization, by Catherine V. McIntyre

The Public Relations Writer's Handbook: The Digital Age, by Merry
   Aronson, Don Spetner and Carol Ames

*The Publicity Handbook: The Inside Scoop from More Than 100
   Journalists and PR Pros on How to Get Great Publicity Coverage*,
   by David R. Yale with Andrew J. Carothers

Perfecting the Pitch: Creating Publicity Through Media Rapport, by
   Benjamin Lewis

Gale Directory of Publications and Broadcast Media

News Media Yellow Book

CDs

The Art of the Press Kit, by Mitchel Whitington

Booking Guest Spots

Radio-TV Interview Report / Bradley Communications:
   www.rtir.com

Press Releases

PR Web Press Release Newswire: www.prweb.com

Send 2 Press: www.send2press.com

Search the Internet on "press release," "press release samples,"
"e-mail press release" and "press release distribution."

Media Training and Image Consulting

Do an Internet search on one of the following + your city.

- media training
- vocal training
- speaker training
- radio training
- image consulting
- voice training
- accent reduction
- broadcast training
- on-camera training
- personal shopper

 FIFTEEN

NETWORKING

The best way to connect with potential clients is through personal contact. Networking, both formal and informal, is a great way to reach your target audience.

BENEFITS

◆ **Connect directly with potential clients and referral sources**

When you select your networking venues strategically, you'll connect with your target audience and/or with people who can lead you to them. (See chapter 16 for more about referral sources.)

◆ **Build mutually beneficial relationships**

Networking is about building professional relationships that are a win-win for all parties. In the best networking relationships, you can give as well as receive.

◆ **Get comfortable with your sales pitch**

By getting out there and telling people what you do on a regular basis, you can refine your message and get more confident and comfortable in sharing it.

GETTING STARTED

Where to Network

While networking is a great way to connect directly with your target audience, it can be time-consuming. Rather than spreading your efforts too thinly, it's important to be selective about your venues, and not try to reach everyone.

Some of the best places to network include:

◆ **Formal leads groups**

These are membership groups that generally include only one representative from each profession, so you're not competing for leads. If the group allows more than one coach, it would be from different niches, such as a Life Coach, a Wellness Coach and a Business Coach. The best-known groups are Business Networking International (BNI) and Le Tip. This type of group can be particularly effective for coaches offering business support.

Do a search for "networking groups" and your city to see what's available. To focus on a particular target audience, you might also include an industry, such as "real estate" or "human resources." Some groups have multiple chapters in larger cities.

◆ **Professional and special-interest organizations and associations**

These may be professional association meetings attended by your target market, as well as special interest groups, such as writing, entrepreneurial or parenting groups. You can also network at coaching organizations. Since coaches operate in so many different niches, you can create alliances with coaches in various niches (even someone in your own niche who takes a different approach), and you can be referral sources for each other. (See also chapter 16.)

◆ **Business meetings and conferences**

This is another great venue for Business Coaches. Look for meetings and conferences with subject matter that is relevant to your target audience, as well as general business and entrepreneurial gatherings. Plan ahead by getting a schedule from your local convention center or Chamber of Commerce, and look for listings in trade and business publications.

◆ **Online networks, aka "social networking"**

With so many of us spending the day in front of our computers, online social networks have become all the rage. These can be very effective in connecting you with potential clients. Some of the more popular ones are LinkedIn, FaceBook, Plaxo, Twitter, MySpace, Ryze and Meetup.

To be most effective, these require regular participation, "linking up" with other people (and thus getting access to *their* network), getting recommendations from satisfied clients and business colleagues who know your work, and posting updates about your professional and personal (be discreet!) activities. These allow people to get to know you through your work, as well as your personal interests.

◆ **Informal networking**

Some people are great at making natural connections as they go about their lives. You're likely to run into compatible clients at places that you typically hang out: adult learning centers, spiritual and religious organizations, men's and women's groups, health clubs and spas, social clubs, special interest groups and classes.

You can also be prepared to "network" with people you run into during the day. When you're standing on that long, boring line at the motor vehicle bureau, you might strike up a conversation with the person next to you on line. This often leads to a discussion of what you do for a living, giving you an opening to talk about coaching and how you help clients, and to give them your business card.

HOW TO NETWORK

Networking is more than just showing up and handing out business cards. Here are a few tips to help you focus your networking.

♦ Before you begin networking, build your strategy. As always, start by defining the type of people you want to connect with. These may be your potential customers, or they may be referral sources who can connect you with your target audience.

♦ Select networking venues that would be beneficial for you. In the beginning, you may need to try some out and see what kind of response you get. Through trial and error, you'll narrow down the venues that bring you the most clients (or other opportunities, such as speaking engagements).

♦ It's important to be able to speak about what you do with confidence. Get clear on what makes you unique and the value you offer — your services, strengths and benefits (see chapter 2) — and then get out there and share it. It may feel uncomfortable at first, but the more you do it, the easier it will get.

Many networkers begin with an "elevator speech" or "sound byte" — a succinct statement of what you offer. This may be something like, "I'm a Career Discovery Coach, and I help stay-at-home moms find new careers and get back into the work force." Or, "I'm a Relationship Coach. I help make good marriages great." Your elevator speech should be short, engaging and stimulate curiosity, leading to further discussion of what you do. (More about this in chapter 2.)

♦ Networking is about quality, not quantity. New networkers often go to meetings and see how many business cards they can exchange. They barely spend enough time with any one person to make any real connection.

♦ Think about what you can give, as well as what you can get. You want to create a relationship that is give-and-take, so that both of you benefit from the connection.

◆ Bring lots of business cards, as well as other materials you have, such as brochures, one-sheets, postcards or promotional items (see chapter 13). You want to give them something to remember you by, but not load them down.

◆ Finally, be sure to get *their* card, so you can follow up with them and solidify the connection. Gathering tons of business cards is a waste of time and energy if you don't follow up and build the relationship. Take the initiative to contact them and to stay in touch; don't depend on them to call you.

EXERCISE
Your Elevator Speech

Write a succinct elevator speech that you can use when introducing yourself at networking events. Make sure it reflects a benefit that you offer and intrigues the listener enough to want to hear more.

What If You're Shy?

All of this can be challenging for a shy person. But as they say, it's the "squeaky wheel" that gets the attention, and coaching sells best when you make personal connections. As a recovered shy person myself, I can tell you that the more you get out and mix with people, the easier it gets.

A tip: While you need to be prepared to talk about what you do, it's more important to be interest*ed* than interest*ing*. People feel more connected when they feel heard. Instead of feeling like you need to dazzle people, focus instead on listening and learning about them.

If networking really goes against the grain with you, then forget about it and work with the many other tools in this book.

RESOURCES

The following resources are offered as suggestions, and NOT recommendations. Internet businesses in particular are notorious for changing. If you are considering using any of these vendors, check them out carefully and make an informed decision.

Books

How to Work a Room: The Ultimate Guide to Savvy Socializing, by Susan RoAne

Make Your Contacts Count: Networking Know-How for Cash, Clients and Career Success, by Anne Baber and Lynne Waymon

Never Eat Alone: And Other Secrets to Success, One Relationship at a Time, by Keith Ferrazzi and Tahl Raz

The Secrets of Savvy Networking: How to Make the Best Connections for Business and Personal Success, by Susan RoAne

Savvy Networking: 118 Fast & Effective Tips for Business Success, by Andrea Nierenberg

Self-Promotion for Introverts: The Quiet Guide to Getting Ahead, by Nancy Ancowitz

Leads Groups

Business Networking International (BNI): www.bni.com

Le Tip: www.letip.com

Networking Groups and Professional Associations

Ladies Who Launch: www.ladieswholaunch.com

National Association of Female Executives: www.nafe.com

National Association of Women Business Owners: www. nawbo.org

Business Organizations (Yahoo): dir.yahoo.com/Business_and_Economy/organizations/professional

Professional Associations (Internet Public Library): www.ipl.org/div/aon

Your local Chamber of Commerce: www.chamberofcommerce.com

Do an Internet search for "networking groups" + your city.

Networking Online (Social Networks)

FaceBook: www.facebook.com

LinkedIn: www.linkedin.com

Meetup: www.meetup.com

MySpace: www.myspace.com

Ning: www.ning.com

Plaxo: www.plaxo.com

Ryze: www.ryze.com

Twitter: www.twitter.com

Xing: www.xing.com

 **SIXTEEN**

REFERRALS AND
STRATEGIC ALLIANCES

Connecting with other professionals is a great way to build your business through mutual support. You may be able to refer clients to each other, or you may provide advice and support. In a solo business like coaching, which can be isolating, having a professional network can be a sanity saver.

BENEFITS

◆ **Get others lined up who will send you clients**

Having others in your court who have exposure to your target clients, and who are willing to send some your way, can make building your business a lot easier.

◆ **Have ongoing business support even if you work alone**

Questions and dilemmas invariably arise during the course of business, and it's helpful to have a trusted peer group (or individuals) to whom you can go to discuss strategies and solutions.

GETTING STARTED

Start by scoping out who might be good referral sources or strategic alliances for you. These may be:

◆ Professional contacts — people you meet within the coaching profession or other business professionals you meet through networking.

◆ Complementary professionals — people in businesses that enhance yours, but who are not in competition with you. For example, Career Coaches might form alliances with resume services or executive recruiting firms; Small Business Coaches might form alliances with accountants and lawyers; Parenting Coaches might form alliances with obstetricians, midwives, teachers and daycare providers.

◆ Personal contacts — people in your personal network who have access to your ideal client type.

◆ Current and former clients — satisfied clients are often willing and eager to refer their friends and colleagues to you.

EXERCISE 1
Exploring Referral Sources

Make a list of the types of professionals who might be good referral sources for you. These might be therapists, lawyers, accountants, personal trainers, health professionals, business professionals, owners of complementary businesses, etc.

Next, list the names of anyone you know in those categories, as well as anyone in your personal or professional network who might connect you with them. Do research to add additional names to your list.

EXERCISE 2
Exploring Strategic Alliances

Make a list of individuals or businesses that might be good alliances for you. Include coaches who are in noncompetitive niches, as well as coaches in the same niche who you might consult with on coaching issues. Also, list organizations where you might network to meet more people who would be good strategic partners (see chapter 15).

∞

HOW TO WORK WITH REFERRALS AND STRATEGIC ALLIANCES

Referrals

In order to establish good referral sources, you want to create relationships with people who have access to your target audience and who are not in competition with you. (See Exercise 1 above.)

Using your list of possible referral sources, select one who you feel would be easy to connect with and/or a good source of referrals. Contact the person and set up a meeting. Tell them about what you do and who you work with. Remember to focus on creating relationship — show an interest in them and their business.

Discuss the possibility of referrals; if you are able to offer referrals to them as well, you can mention that. Leave a stack of business cards or brochures (and get theirs if you can also refer clients to them). Send a thank-you note, and then keep in touch. E-mail an interesting article or let them know when you're doing a workshop. Be sure to thank them with a note or small gift when they send you clients.

Remember, you can also exchange referrals with coaches in other niches, or those in your own niche who have a different approach or a different target audience.

EXERCISE
Establishing Referral Sources

Begin contacting referral sources. Start with two or three. Be sure to keep in touch with those sources with whom you've made a positive connection. Continue courting referral sources until you have a good, steady stream of clients coming to you.

∞

Strategic Alliances

Alliances may be generated deliberately or may arise spontaneously. You can invite a small group of compatible professionals to join you in a mastermind group (see below), or you may "click" with fellow professionals you meet while networking.

Set up regular meetings to discuss business issues and enjoy each other's company (and get out of the office!). Even with a compatible group that forms naturally, you have to be proactive to maintain the connection. People are busy, so you need to get some meetings on the calendar. It's best to meet at least every four to six weeks to keep the momentum going. And, of course, you can always call on each other between meetings when you need support on a specific issue.

You might also want to do business together. You can develop workshops or products or co-write a book, and you can use your coaching skills to keep each other on track and motivated with your respective businesses.

Mastermind Groups

The concept of mastermind groups comes from Napoleon Hill's book, *Think and Grow Rich*. A mastermind group consists of a handful of entrepreneurs who meet on a regular basis to support each other with the success of their businesses. Your group may consist only of coaches, or you can open it to other types of entrepreneurs.

Carefully select the members of your group. Since you will be sharing confidential information, you want to work with people you trust. Keep your meetings focused by creating an agenda, so that each person's needs are taken care of. If you enjoy each other's company, you can complete the meeting by socializing over a meal, but make sure you complete the business first.

Coaching Companies

While coaching is often a solo business, some coaches prefer to be affiliated with a company, rather than doing all their marketing and business building on their own. As the coaching profession evolves, coaching companies are starting to spring up. These may be companies that hire coaches and provide coaching services to companies and/or individuals, or they may subcontract with individual coaches and provide referrals for a commission. You can find these companies through the Internet or by networking. Some corporations also hire "internal coaches" to work with their executives and staff.

In addition, individual coaches are banding together and forming companies, so that they can share in their marketing efforts and support each other in building their businesses. These alliances are best found by networking with coaches through local coaching groups and business networking meetings, until you find people you feel compatible with.

EXERCISE
Establishing Strategic alliances

Invite a group of compatible professionals to join you in a mastermind group, or attend networking meetings with the intention of connecting with potential group members. Create an agenda and start meeting on a regular basis.

RESOURCES

The following resources are offered as suggestions, and NOT recommendations. Internet businesses in particular are notorious for changing. If you are considering using any of these vendors, check them out carefully and make an informed decision.

Books

Referrals

Business by Referral: A Sure-Fire Way to Generate New Business, by Ivan Misner

Get More Referrals Now!, by Bill Cates

The Official Guide to Building a Referral Based Business, by Cezar Mansour

Strategic Alliances

Alliance Advantage: The Art of Creating Value Through Partnering, by Yves L. Doz and Gary Hamel

Developing Strategic Alliances, by Ed Rigsbee

Meet and Grow Rich: How to Easily Create and Operate Your Own "Mastermind" Group for Health, Wealth, and More, by Joe Vitale and Bill Hibbler

Strategic Partnerships: An Entrepreneur's Guide to Joint Ventures and Alliances, by Robert Wallace

 **Seventeen**

Closing Notes

Now that you've got the full picture of all the different ways you can market, I'd like to end with some thoughts to help you make good choices and pull it all together.

Make Your Marketing Strategy Your Own

As you get out into the world of marketing, you're going to hear a lot of experts tell you what you *should* do. Many of them will direct you toward a six-figure practice and selling, selling, selling. Some people love that. For others, it will feel forced and inauthentic, and you will be miserable and overwhelmed if you try to keep up that pace.

It's important to evaluate your own goals for yourself and your business. As you go about designing your marketing strategy, consider the following questions.

♦ **What feels natural to you?**

You need to do your marketing in a way that works for you. If you try to go against your own nature, your prospects will sense your discomfort. Better to turn down the intensity of your marketing and do it authentically.

◆ What does your ideal practice look like?

There's a lot of pressure in the business world to constantly grow bigger and make more money. Other coaches will ask: How many clients do you have? or, Do you have a full practice yet? You may feel embarrassed to respond if you're not able to live up to their expectations.

Don't cave in to this outer pressure. Take the time to envision what *your* ideal practice will look like. Sure, everyone wants to make tons of money, but how much do you really need to support the lifestyle *you* want? How hard are you willing to work for it, and what are you willing to sacrifice? Do you really *want* a full-time practice, or do you want to combine it with other types of work, raising a family, volunteering, more leisure time or other activities that are important to you?

◆ How much can you handle?

In envisioning your ideal practice, it's important to take into account how much you can handle, not just how much you want to make. New coaches may look at their financial goals and target 20 to 30 clients a week, without realizing how much energy it takes to work with each client, as well as the paperwork and marketing that go into supporting your practice.

As you work with clients, get a feel for how many appointments you can realistically handle in a day. We're not all Energizer Bunnies®, and you may need to limit the size of your practice in order to honor your needs and not burn out. Remember — as coaches, we need to walk our talk. You don't want to be hustling and working so much that you're exhausted and unhealthy and your life is out of balance. That's not going to present an appealing picture to potential clients.

◆ **What do you need to have in place?**

As you plan your transition into your coaching practice, think about your business "infrastructure." Consider which of the following you may need:

- **Cash reserves.** You want to make sure you're responsibly taking care of your finances. Prospective clients can sense when you're desperate. As you're building your new business, you'll need to invest in training and marketing, as well as continuing to pay your bills. If you can hang onto your day job, or transition to part time while you build your practice, so much the better. It also doesn't hurt to have enough in a savings account to support yourself for 6 to 12 months , so you have a cushion to fall back on.

- **A support system**. Starting a new business is challenging. It can roller coaster from exhilarating to discouraging. You need support from family, friends, a coach or business alliances (see chapter 16). Don't isolate yourself and try to go it alone. When you feel supported, you're more likely to succeed.

- **Other income streams.** As you begin to build your coaching practice, you may discover that you want to have a part-time coaching practice and continue working part-time in your old profession (or a different one) or have other coaching-related income streams, such as teaching, consulting or product lines. Be honest about what you really want, and don't let yourself be intimidated by the question, How many clients do you have?

◆ **How can you include yourself in your marketing?**

In his book, *Personality Not Included,* social media guru Rohit Bhargava tells us that in the 21st century, even large corporations need to have a dynamic personality in order to attract customers (note aforementioned Energizer Bunny®, as well as the adorable Geico gecko).

As individual practitioners, whose business depends on making a personal connection with our clients, having a presence in your market is crucial. As you design your website and other marketing materials, make sure that you authentically share your personality and passion, so that you attract clients who will connect with you. Go back and review the chapters in section I for tips on how to do that.

Creating Your Strategy

To begin strategizing your marketing plan, make a copy of appendix F. In the first column, rate each marketing tool based on its level of appeal for you. The ones you like best would be rated "1". Other tools that interest you would be rated "2". Any tool that you have no interest in would be rated "3" (or leave it blank).

Next, select one to three tools to begin with. Ideally, select from the tools you rated "1". In some cases, there may be a tool that doesn't particularly interest you, but that's strategically important, such as a website or opening a Facebook account. Prioritize the rest of your favored tools in the order in which you'd like to implement them, either individually or in groupings.

Finally, for each tool, write an action plan. List the steps you need to take, and set a target date for completing each step. You may want to work on two or three tools simultaneously, or roll them out one at a time.

If marketing is challenging for you, get a support system. Work with a mentor coach or a peer group to hold you accountable and bolster your confidence. (See chapter 16 for more on strategic alliances.)

Work with the Principles of Attraction

There's a lot of talk these days about the Law of Attraction. While that may sound a bit "out there," there are some simple, practical steps you can take to use it to your advantage in attracting clients.

◆ Be clear about what you want

Use the questions above to clarify what you want your coaching practice to look like. When you're clear and confident about what you want, and you've confronted the doubts and fears head-on, you're much more likely to manifest your vision.

◆ Know the value of what you offer

Many new coaches feel uncomfortable charging the rates that are common in coaching, which may feel high compared to what you've earned in your previous careers. Or you may feel concern that you're still building your skill as a coach and find it hard to present yourself with confidence. You may know intellectually that coaching is valuable to clients, but you may find it difficult to relate that general concept to yourself.

Get clear on the skills and strengths you bring to your work as a coach, including past professional and personal experiences that add to your value. As you work with clients, keep a list of their successes and the impact that your coaching has had on their lives, or ask them to give you feedback. When you feel insecure, go back and read that list.

◆ Share your enthusiasm

When you authentically share your passion about coaching, you don't have to "sell." People will feel your enthusiasm and naturally become curious about this fabulous thing you're doing.

◆ Build your confidence

Along with being persistent with my marketing efforts and building momentum, I found that as I became more confident in my skill and ability as a coach, more people began calling me to inquire about coaching, and more signed on. I began to get more clients with less effort. To build your confidence, keep practicing and working with clients consistently, even if it's pro bono. Have your clients give you feedback and testimonials.

◆ Come from a place of abundance

When I began coaching, one of the things I loved about the profession was the generosity of the senior coaches, who were willing to share tips and encourage me. When you come from a place of abundance and generosity, the Universe "gets" that there are more than enough clients for everyone. Take care of your own business, but be generous and share when you can.

◆ **Have a clear intention and take action**

The key to the Law of Attraction is to have a clear intention about what you want, focus your attention on that (rather than on what you *don't* want), take actions toward that vision and behave as if you're already successful. All four steps are important.

◆ **Be persistent and don't give up**

No matter how talented you are, if you give up when the going gets rough, you'll never see your vision come to fruition. Get clear on what you want (allowing for flexibility as new opportunities open up to you); make sure your basic needs are taken care of, so you don't approach new clients with an air of desperation; and just keep going until you reach your goal.

Work smart, not hard

As you work on marketing and building your practice, use your resources efficiently. Start small. Try out different marketing tools. See which ones work for you, and focus your time and attention on those. Build momentum. As your practice grows, you'll spend more time coaching and less marketing.

Remember that coaching is an idea whose time has come. We have a valuable service to offer, and the world needs us. Connect with other coaches, so you don't feel isolated as you build your business.

Finally, go out there and make your life great. We're all works in progress, but the more you practice what you preach, the more clients will be drawn to you naturally. So, have fun, be the inspiration you are and do great!

APPENDIX A: SAMPLE PLAIN-TEXT NEWSLETTER

"Living the Creative Life" is published monthly. You are receiving this e-newsletter because you subscribed at our website or at Topica.com or requested to be subscribed. You may also receive occasional special mailings. We will not share your e-mail address with any third party.

To access this newsletter on the web, click on these links:
http://www.goodlifecoaching.com/CreativeLife97.html
http://www.goodlifecoaching.com/Classes.html
http://www.goodlifepress.com

^^

LIVING THE CREATIVE LIFE
^^^^^^^^^^^^^^^^^^^^^^^^^^^^^^^^

For Creative People
and Those Who Want To
Live Their Lives Creatively

^^

February 2008 ~ ~ ~ Issue 97

In this issue ~~
* Opening Notes
* Feature Article: WHO DO YOU WANT TO BECOME?
* Action Challenge
* Wise Words
* Bookshelf
* Upcoming Classes with Sharon
    - In NYC: Coaching Classes at NYU
    - In NYC: What to Do When You Don't Know What to Do
    ~ Teleseminar: Life Purpose Institute Coach Certification Training

^^^

OPENING NOTES

Now that the new year seems a distant memory, it's time to think about our next steps. The glow of our resolutions is beginning to wear off, and we need to evaluate what we're really committed to.

One way that I assess my next steps is by looking at what's next in my own development. As much as I love getting comfortable with what I'm doing, there's a part of me that craves challenge and is always looking for the next opportunity to stretch.

I hope you enjoy this issue's article and that it spurs you to think about new ways to determine what *your* next steps might be!

Creatively yours,
Sharon

^^^

WHO DO YOU WANT TO BECOME?

Growing and changing is a natural part of our human development. We know this. When we're thinking about what's next for us, though, we tend to look back at our history to see what the next logical step is. But we may have dreams and passions we want to pursue that are not a linear outcome of what we've done before, so they don't feel doable. What do we do then?

Instead of creating our future out of our past, we can look at who we want to become. Usually, when we're looking toward our future, we think about what we want to *do*. But what about looking at who we want to *be*? Life is not just a string of accomplishments. It's a process in which we gain knowledge and experience and develop who we are.

When I was younger, I didn't think much about who I was becoming. I knew I wanted to be an actress from the age of 14, and I didn't care why. I pursued that path without further thought until I was in my 30s and found myself on a path of personal and spiritual growth. The question,

How can I best serve? began to creep into my mind. While I realized that actors perform an important service, it wasn't the right kind of service for me anymore.

My next step was a foray into the world of publishing. I had no background in this field, but it was an opportunity to develop my writing skill and publish books that brought valuable tools and information and heart-warming stories into the world. It was a huge challenge to run a business and be responsible for bookkeeping and marketing and inventory. I grew tremendously and was proud of the books we published, but eventually, it ran its course and a new opportunity arose.

After 7 years of publishing, I happened upon an article about life coaching. We were still in the thick of publishing, and I certainly didn't need another career, but it kept tugging at me. After completing what turned out to be our last book, I enrolled in a coach training course. I loved it! This wonderful new profession – my new "best way to serve" – continues to allow me to have an even more direct, positive impact on people's lives. In working with my clients, as well as teaching and writing, I learn and grow every day.

In looking back, my career path makes a lot of sense. My acting experience has helped make me a better teacher and speaker. I continue to write and publish self-help materials that support my coaching focus. But as I began each new career, I had no idea why I was drawn to it or what it would bring. I only knew that I needed to step into a new challenge that would develop who I was as a person and a professional.

As we move to each new stage of life, a new sense of purpose is revealed to us. The things we did and who we were become a size too small, and we need to break out and seek new direction. It may be the logical next step from what we've been doing, or it may be a radical change. Either way, our new path calls on us to be willing to let go of the comfort of the old, familiar ways and open to learning new skills and new ways of being.

In the words of Shunryo Suzuki-Roshi, a 20th century Japanese Zen priest: "In the beginner's mind there are many possibilities, but in the expert's there are few." Although you may have decades of life experience behind you, approach your new stage with beginner's mind.

By letting go of relying on what you already know – about life and about yourself – you'll discover wonderful new aspects of yourself that will move you forward in your development, as well as your accomplishments, and open new worlds. And down the line, when the time is right, yet another new and mysterious path will be revealed to you!

~~~~~~

ACTION CHALLENGE

~~~~~~~~~~~~~~~~~~~~~

Make a list of at least 10 adjectives that describe who you want to become in the next 5 to 10 years. Take one of these adjectives. What steps can you take in the next month to become more of that? In the next year?

WISE WORDS

~~~~~~~~~~~~~

"The highest reward for a person's toil is not what they get for it, but what they become by it."

~ John Ruskin

"Growth demands a temporary surrender of security."

~ Gail Sheehy

"I began to have an idea of my life, not as the slow shaping of achievement to fit my preconceived purposes, but as the gradual discovery and growth of a purpose which I did not know."

~ Joanna Field

BOOKSHELF

~~~~~~~~~~~~~~

"Who Am I?: The 16 Basic Desires That Motivate Our Actions and Define Our Personalities" . . . Steven Reiss, PhD
http://www.amazon.com/exec/obidos/ISBN=0425183408/sharongoodlifeco

"I Think, Therefore Who Am I?" . . . Peter Weissman
http://www.amazon.com/exec/obidos/ISBN=1425702937/sharongoodlifeco

"Driven: How Human Nature Shapes Our Choices" . . . Paul R. Lawrence & Nitin Nohria
http://www.amazon.com/exec/obidos/ISBN=0787963852/sharongoodlifeco

"Who Are You?: 101 Ways of Seeing Yourself" . . . Malcolm Godwin
http://www.amazon.com/exec/obidos/ISBN=0140196099/sharongoodlifeco

"The Temperament Discovery System" . . . David M. Keirsey, Richard Milner, Vince Wood
http://www.amazon.com/exec/obidos/ISBN=1885705042/sharongoodlifeco

"Are You Ready to Succeed?: Unconventional Strategies to Achieving Personal Mastery in Business and Life" . . . Srikumar S. Rao
http://www.amazon.com/exec/obidos/ISBN=1401301932/sharongoodlifeco

"Transitions: Making Sense of Life's Changes" . . . William Bridges
http://www.amazon.com/exec/obidos/ISBN=073820904X/sharongoodlifeco

"Passages: Predictable Crises of Adult Life" . . . Gail Sheehy
http://www.amazon.com/exec/obidos/ISBN=34547922X/sharongoodlifeco

"The Second Half of Life: Opening the Eight Gates of Wisdom" . . . Angeles Arrien
http://www.amazon.com/exec/obidos/ISBN=1591795729/sharongoodlifeco

"Second Acts: Creating the Life You Really Want, Building the Career You Truly Desire" . . . Stephen M. Pollan & Mark Levine
http://www.amazon.com/exec/obidos/ISBN=0060514884/sharongoodlifeco

^^

UPCOMING CLASSES WITH SHARON

~~~~~~~~~~~~~~~~~~~~~~~~~~~~~~~~~~

FOR MORE INFORMATION ON ALL CLASSES, please visit www.goodlifecoaching.com/Classes.html.

~ ~ ~ ~ ~

FOR THOSE IN NEW YORK CITY . . .

COACHING CLASSES AT NEW YORK UNIVERSITY

* CAREER COACHING:

Spring 2008 semester: 2 Saturdays, March 8 and 29, 9 am – 5 pm

* CREATIVE MARKETING TOOLS FOR COACHES:

Spring 2008 semester: 6 Mondays, April 7 to May 12, 6 – 8 pm

For information and registration links, go to www.goodlifecoaching.com/Classes.html.

~ ~ ~

WHAT TO DO WHEN YOU DON'T KNOW WHAT TO DO

So many people are dissatisfied with their jobs or careers. They'd love to get out but they don't know where to go or how to get there. Learn how to uncover new career possibilities and take the first steps in finding a career that will make you happy.

Investment: $25

Location: 92nd Street Y, 1395 Lexington Avenue, NYC

Date and time: Monday, May 19, 7 - 9 PM

To register or get further information, please contact the 92nd Street Y at 212-415-5500. Register online at www.92y.org (course # T-LP5SP55-02).

~ ~ ~ ~ ~ ~ ~

TELESEMINAR . . .

LIFE PURPOSE INSTITUTE COACH CERTIFICATION TAINING

The Life Purpose Institute offers a short-term, focused coach certification program in the format of a 17-week teleseminar. In this program, you'll learn 20 Coaching Skills and the 7-Step Model for Clarity and Results, a powerful toolkit for helping your clients achieve clarity on their life and career goals. In a small group setting (6 to 8 students), you'll practice coaching with the support of your instructor and receive personalized support on preparing your unique marketing strategy for your coaching business.

Sharon Good is a Senior Instructor for the Life Purpose Institute. She will be starting a new teleseminar class on Wednesday, February 27. The class meets weekly for 17 weeks from 6 to 8 pm Pacific time (9 to 11 pm Eastern time).

For additional information, and to sign up for a free introductory phone class, go to www.lifepurposeinstitute.com or phone 858-484-3400.

^^

Sharon Good is a Life/Career/Creativity Coach, Workshop Leader and Author. Her books include "Managing With A Heart: 222 Ways To Make Your Employees Feel Appreciated," "The Tortoise Workbook: Strategies for Getting Ahead at Your Own Pace," and "Self-Publishing Basics."

Sharon is available for one-on-one coaching for:
* whole life balance using the Whole Life model
* successful career and life transitions with the Life Purpose Process©
* support in achieving your goals and dreams
* guidance in writing or publishing your book
* developing your creativity
* enhancing and integrating spirituality in your daily life
* mentoring and practice-building for coaches

For a **COMPLIMENTARY INTRODUCTORY PHONE SESSION**, contact Sharon at 212-564-2073 or sharon@goodlifecoaching.com.

For further information, see her website at http://www.goodlifecoaching.com.

^^

Subscribe & Unsubscribe
~~~~~~~~~~~~~~~~~~~~~~~~

Please feel free to forward a copy of this newsletter to your friends.

To subscribe, go to <http://www.topica.com/lists/creativelife> or send a blank e-mail to <creativelife-subscribe@topica.com>.

To unsubscribe, go to <http://www.topica.com/lists/creativelife> or send a blank e-mail to <creativelife-unsubscribe@topica.com>.

Past issues can be viewed at <http://www.goodlifecoaching.com/CreativeLife.html> or at <http://www.topica.com/lists/creativelife>.

^^

Sharon Good, CC / Good Life Coaching Inc.

Life, Career and Creativity Coach

Certified Life Purpose Process© Consultant

"Being a Tortoise in a World of Hares"

New York, NY 10036

sharon@goodlifecoaching.com

www.goodlifecoaching.com

www.beingatortoise.com

www.goodlifepress.com

"Making your dreams a reality through partnership"

^^

APPENDIX B: FORM FOR COMPARING INTERNET PUBLISHERS

Book specs: Number of pages: _____ Trim size: _____ x _____

	Publisher / Package	Publisher / Package

BASIC PACKAGE FEE
What's included:
  # of free books
  Distribution
  Level of support		

Cost for additional books		
Royalty rate and frequency of payment		
Color printing available?		
ADDITIONAL SERVICES Individualized support		
Copyediting / proofreading		
Custom book cover Upgraded back cover (text, photo)		
Indexing		
Translation		
CD insert		
Copyright registration		
Library of Congress control number		

MARKETING & DISTRIBUTION
  Promotional materials
  Domain name
  E-book distributon
  Amazon look-inside set-up
  Google listing, etc.		

APPENDIX C: SAMPLE WORKSHOP PROPOSAL
Cover Letter

[Your Letterhead]

August 30, 2008

John Smith
My Local Adult Learning Center
400 Main Street
My Town, ST 11111

Dear John,

It was a pleasure speaking with you last week about doing a workshop at MLALC in Spring 2009. Following is a proposal for a workshop that I would like to offer: "Finding Work You Love and Loving the Work You Have." Included are a course description, proposed flyer copy and my bio.

This workshop offers a great opportunity for exploration for those who are considering a career change or just seeking to breathe new life into their current career. Based on your previous catalog offerings, I believe this would be an appropriate focus for the audience you attract.

This workshop is designed to run 2 to 3 hours and would be appropriate for an evening or half-day event. If there is a demand for a longer workshop, it can be expanded into a 3-part workshop, to be given over 3 weeks, that would go more in depth into the process and give participants a chance to work with some of the components and move forward in the process with my continued guidance.

Please let me know if you have any questions or need any additional supporting materials. I will call you next week to discuss our next steps.

Sincerely,

Sharon Good

Attachments: Course Description, Catalog/Flyer Copy, Instructor Bio

Course Description

FINDING WORK YOU LOVE AND LOVING THE WORK YOU HAVE

Instructor: Sharon Good

In today's world of downsizing, reengineering and lay-offs, with job security no longer a given, many people are realizing that work is about more than money. Job satisfaction and a balanced life are important, and many people are leaving unsatisfying jobs to pursue their dreams. And those who have been in a career they enjoy for many years are looking for ways to revitalize it, bringing new challenges and excitement.

But so many people have lost touch with their dreams. After so many years of being told what's correct for our gender, economic bracket, education, etc., we've forgotten who we are and what really matters to us. We've gotten in the habit of just getting through the day, and lost touch with how it's draining our energy.

In this workshop, we will go through a series of individualized self-exploration exercises that will help each participant get in touch with what they love and enjoy, what really matters to them, their values, as well as their practical needs. The process goes on to help them put the various pieces together to find a work path that will bring them a sense of satisfaction and purpose, whether this means finding a job or starting a business.

In this evening workshop, instructor Sharon Good will:

- Dialog with participants about what brings meaning to their life
- Begin the self-exploration process by guiding participants through several exercises to help them get back in touch with what they love
- Open their vision to new possibilities and look at the concept of work with new eyes
- Begin to synthesize the components to design a new career or find ways to revitalize the one they have

Participants will leave the workshop:

- With some concrete ideas of what matters to them and some career possibilities
- With a new perspective on work and on their work
- Feeling inspired and empowered to continue their search

Note: This evening workshop can be extended to 3 sessions, in which participants go deeper into the process with the guidance of the instructor.

Catalog/Flyer Copy

FINDING WORK YOU LOVE AND LOVING THE WORK YOU HAVE

with Sharon Good

Are you dissatisfied with your work life? Have you ever longed to be doing work you loved, but thought of it as a distant dream? Do you feel there's something more out there awaiting you? Do you want to feel that your work is meaningful to yourself and others? Do you want to breathe new life into the work you're doing? If you answered "YES" to at least one of these questions, come join us for an experiential workshop designed to help you reignite your passion and find work you love or infuse your current work with new life.

Sharon Good is a certified Life and Career Coach with over 10 years' experience helping clients find careers and designing lives they love. In this workshop, through discussion and exercises, Sharon will guide you to:

- Get back in touch with your passion
- Learn to look at work in a new way
- Discover what's involved in finding your perfect work
- Look at what's getting in your way
- Create an action plan

So, whether this is your first career change or your fifth, or if you simply want to enjoy what you're already doing, you can design a career you love. Join Sharon, and get on the road to career fulfillment!

Instructor Bio

Sharon Good is President of Good Life Coaching Inc. and a Life, Career and Creativity Coach based in New York City. Sharon helps people create fulfilling lives and find work they love using the Life Purpose Process©. A graduate of Hofstra University, she is certified in Life and Career Coaching by the Life Purpose Institute and holds a certificate in Adult Career Planning and Development from New York University. With her background in publishing, theatre, photography and computers, she helps artists achieve their creative goals and assists writers in getting published or self-publishing their work.

A former Director of the New York City chapter of the International Coach Federation, Sharon coaches individuals and groups from all walks of life to create a life they love and achieve their goals. As co-owner of Excalibur Publishing for 16 years, she published and edited numerous books and is the author of several books, including *Managing With A Heart: 222 Ways to Make Your Employees Feel Appreciated* and *The Tortoise Workbook: Strategies for Getting Ahead at Your Own Pace*, as well as her e-newsletter, *Living the Creative Life*.

Sharon trains coaches for the Life Purpose Institute and is an adjunct instructor in the coaching program at New York University. She has taught workshops and teleclasses for the 92nd Street Y, Bronxville Adult School, the Learning Annex, the Career Change Network, the Virtual Reality Self-Help Center, Axxess Business Centers and WriteDirections.com, and has presented for the International Coach Federation/NYC Chapter, the Independent Women's Business Circle, WorkTalk™, the International Facility Management Association, Friends of the Institute of Noetic Sciences and the Network of Enterprising Women. Sharon is an Affiliated Coach with VocationVacations and mentors college students through the Hofstra Career Alumni Advisor Network.

APPENDIX D: SAMPLE WORKSHOP CHECKLIST

Workshop Title _____

Date and Time _____

Location _____

Sponsoring Organization _____

____ Teaching notes

____ Handouts

____ Laptop and PowerPoint presentation

____ Audio-visual equipment / slides / overheads

____ Books or other resource materials

____ Nametags

____ Pens and markers

____ Pad

____ Business cards and brochures

____ Products to sell and order forms

____ Interest surveys

____ Newsletter sign-up

____ Special offers

____ Giveaways

____ Water

APPENDIX E: SAMPLE PRESS RELEASE

There are many variations on press release formats. The format below incorporates many of the expected components and is formatted for e-mail distribution. For additional options, explore the Resources for chapter 14.

FOR IMMEDIATE RELEASE

Massive Layoffs Lead Desperate Former Employees to Seek Out Career Coaches

NEW YORK, NY, October 9, 2008 – Despite a tenuous economy, many downsized employees are seeking out Career Coaches to help them revitalize their careers. Sharon Good, President of Good Life Coaching Inc., says that Career Coaches help job seekers find new jobs or career paths faster and more effectively than they could on their own.

With all the changes in the job market over the past decades, job seekers are challenged to be more creative in their approach, whether they want a new job in their current field or to make a radical career change. Ms. Good works with the Life Purpose Process©, created by Fern Gorin and the Life Purpose Institute, to help individuals to creatively design a fulfilling new career path.

Ms. Good explains: "The Life Purpose Process honors each individual's unique gifts and talents, as well as taking into account their transferable skills and practical needs. Exciting options can emerge from the process. Clients complete the process with a clear direction and a clear plan, which maximizes their chances of success."

Ms. Good coached John Smith, a former broker with ABC Finance, to revive a long-held passion for gardening and turn it into a career as a landscape designer. Alice Jones, a former VP with XYZ Bank, has reinvented herself as a college professor, using her skills in finance to instruct MBA candidates at Pleasantville University.

For many, particularly those who are unemployed, Career Coaching can seem like a big expense. Ms. Good suggests that making this investment helps job seekers get on the right path and find a new job more quickly. Because they begin receiving income sooner, most people can recoup the investment in coaching in the first week or two of employment and still come out ahead.

To learn more about Sharon Good and Career Coaching with the Life Purpose Process, go to: http://www.goodlifecoaching.com/LifePurpose.html

About Good Life Coaching

Good Life Coaching Inc. is a Life and Career Coaching service founded by Sharon Good in 1997. Sharon is a certified Life, Career and Creativity Coach, specializing in helping all types of people to creatively design a life and career that brings them joy. Drawing on her background in theatre, photography, graphic design, writing and publishing, she supports artists in bringing more of their creative work into their lives and starting or making their creative business more profitable and enjoyable.

For more information, visit http://www.goodlifecoaching.com.

CONTACT: Sharon Good, CC – Life, Career & Creativity Coach
President, Good Life Coaching Inc.
E-mail: sharon@goodlifecoaching.com
Phone: 212-564-2073
Web: www.goodlifecoaching.com

###

If you'd like more information about this topic, or to schedule an interview with Sharon Good, please call 212-564-2073 or e-mail sharon@goodlifecoaching.com.

APPENDIX F: MY CREATIVE MARKETING STRATEGY

Step 1: Rate each of the marketing tools as follows: 1 = most appealing; 2 = somewhat appealing; 3 = no interest (or leave blank).

Step 2: Number the tools in the order in which you want to implement them. You may work on two or three simultaneously, but be careful of launching too many at the same time.

	Appeal	Order
Websites	_____	_____
E-zines / newsletters	_____	_____
Blogs	_____	_____
Podcasts	_____	_____
Articles	_____	_____
Books / e-books	_____	_____
Audios	_____	_____
Videos	_____	_____
Speaking	_____	_____
Workshops	_____	_____
Promotional materials	_____	_____
Media	_____	_____
Networking	_____	_____
Referrals	_____	_____

Coaching with Sharon

Individual Coaching

Sharon Good has coached individuals on life, career and creativity issues since 1997. She coaches both in person and by phone, and her clients include individuals from all over the United States and internationally.

For more information about Sharon, her coaching philosophy and the types of clients she works best with, visit her website at www.goodlifecoaching.com. To schedule a free introductory phone consultation, contact Sharon at sharon@goodlifecoaching.com.

Coach Training at The Life Purpose Institute

Along with individual coaching, Sharon trains coaches for the Life Purpose Institute. Since 1984, the Life Purpose Institute has offered the most personal coach training available. Both the 17-week phone class and the 5-day on-site intensive feature small classes with a lot of personal attention, to offer trainees the best opportunities to learn coaching techniques and develop their skills with the supervision of a senior instructor.

For more information about the Life Purpose Institute, including the current class schedule, and to sign up for a free introductory teleseminar, visit their website at www.lifepurposeinstitute.com.

About the Author

Sharon Good is President of Good Life Coaching Inc. and a Life, Career and Creativity Coach based in New York City. Sharon helps people create fulfilling lives and find work they love using the Life Purpose Process©. A graduate of Hofstra University, she is certified in Life and Career Coaching by the Life Purpose Institute and holds a certificate in Adult Career Planning and Development from New York University. Sharon coaches individuals and groups from all walks of life to create a life they love and achieve their goals. With her background in publishing, performing, photography and graphic design, she helps artists achieve their creative goals and assists writers in getting published or self-publishing their work.

As co-owner of Excalibur Publishing for 16 years, Sharon published and edited numerous books. She is the author of several books, including *Managing With A Heart: 222 Ways to Make Your Employees Feel Appreciated* and *The Tortoise Workbook: Strategies for Getting Ahead at Your Own Pace*, as well as her e-newsletter, *Living the Creative Life*. She continues to publish her work through her new publishing company, Good Life Press (www.goodlifepress.com).

Sharon trains coaches for the Life Purpose Institute and is an adjunct instructor in the coaching program at New York University's School of Continuing and Professional Studies. She has taught workshops and teleclasses for the 92nd Street Y, Bronxville Adult School, the Learning Annex, the Career Change Network, the Virtual Reality Self-Help Center and Axxess Business Centers, among many others; has been a guest instructor at Columbia University and the Fashion Institute of Technology; and has presented for the International Coach Federation/NYC Chapter, the Independent Women's Business Circle, WorkTalk™, Friends of the Institute of Noetic Sciences and the Network of Enterprising Women. Sharon is proud to be an Affiliated Coach with VocationVacations.

Sharon can be reached via her websites: www.goodlifecoaching.com, www.goodlifepress.com and www.beingatortoise.com.